MAKE THEM
THINK

How to coach for OWNERSHIP,
INSIGHT *and* ACTION

JENN FARRER

COPYRIGHT

Make Them Think: How To Coach for Ownership, Insight, and Action

© 2026 by Jennifer Farrer.

Printed in the United States of America

First Edition, 2026

ISBN: 979-8-9945847-0-5

Author: Jenn Farrer

Publisher: Jennifer Farrer

Website: www.jenniferfarrer.com

DEDICATION

This book is dedicated to everyone who wants to help others change their lives for the better.

Thank you for being here. The world needs more people like you.

~

To Ben and Max, thank you for always making me think and helping me grow.

PROLOGUE

By the time I reached kindergarten, my teacher walked me to my mom's car every afternoon with the same report: "We got another frowny face today." I had spent the day watching the other kids instead of doing my assignment. I couldn't help it. People fascinated me. How they talked to each other, what made them laugh, why some kids played together and others sat alone. As an only child who moved around a lot, watching people was how I learned to navigate the world.

My parents had both grown up in small rural towns in Virginia before eventually landing in Richmond, where I grew up. My mom returned to teaching high school math when I started kindergarten. My dad worked in the restaurant business, then became a mail carrier. They believed every generation should do better than the one before it, and I took that to heart. Grades mattered. Getting into a good college mattered. Landing a job that paid well mattered. I absorbed all of it.

So I learned to achieve. By 26, I was a full-blown Type A workaholic. I pushed myself in every direction: to be pretty, to be thin, to have the best job, to make as much money as possible. I always had several entrepreneurial ventures running alongside my full-time corporate job. I didn't know any other way to live.

Then something happened that changed the trajectory of my life.

I was in Manhattan on a cold November morning, walking through Midtown on a coffee run with my boyfriend of two months. My head was spinning, my equilibrium off. I assumed it was the worst hangover of my life. Back in our hotel room, lazing in bed, it hit. What doctors call a "thunderclap headache," though that term doesn't capture it. My vision went black. The throbbing was so severe that snot poured from my nose and tears streamed down my face. I could hear everything going on around me, but I couldn't form words to speak. I heard Ben asking what was happening; Ben on the phone with 911; the paramedics asking what medications I was on. But I couldn't respond. I heard him tell them I was on birth control pills when actually I had just started NuvaRing. I tried to correct him. My mouth wouldn't move.

The hospital gave me Percocet and sent me home with the diagnosis of "my first migraine."

For three weeks, I lay in my childhood bed at my mom's house in Richmond while doctors cycled through misdiagnoses. Migraines. Encephalitis. I swallowed painkillers and waited. Then my legs started going numb. I'd be walking and suddenly there was nothing from the knees down. I'd collapse. Finally, a neurologist got me in for more tests. I was at my mom's house when he called.

"I need you to stay calm when I tell you this," he said. "The scan shows collapsed blood vessels in your brain and a small bleed. I want you to go to St. Mary's Hospital and check yourself into the ICU. I'll meet you there."

For eleven days, I lay in the ICU. There was nothing to do but wait for the bleeding to stop. I had a subarachnoid hemorrhage, a type of stroke with a dim prognosis. The doctors explained my odds of survival, then my odds of surviving without lasting damage. I had been an avid runner. Now I couldn't walk. I thought of my mom, who had lost my dad to cancer eighteen months earlier. As an only child, I couldn't bear the thought of leaving her alone. I thought of Ben, only 24, sitting in the waiting room with my mom. Two people who had just met, holding vigil together.

I remember thinking that I'd have to dump Ben because he was too kind to leave me. I couldn't saddle a man in his twenties with a wheelchair-bound girlfriend for life.

I went home on December 18th. My mom hadn't decorated for Christmas yet. She put up a tree for my homecoming, and we invited a few of my high school friends over. I couldn't look directly at the tree. The lights were too blurry, like headlights hitting a dirty windshield at night.

I did walk again. I ran again. In 2013, I completed the New York City Marathon.

But the bigger change wasn't physical. That stroke rewrote my relationship with time. I had lost my dad when I was 24 and he was 60. Now I had almost died at 26. The math was clear: we don't have as much time as we think, and I was done wasting mine on work, people, and pursuits that didn't mean anything to me.

I left my corporate job, moved to DC to be with Ben, and eventually earned a graduate degree in communication, researching how people actually influence each other and change. I joined Gallup's management consulting practice, became a certified executive coach, trained in mindfulness-based stress reduction, and started my own coaching practice. Along the way, I became a running coach too, because running, I had discovered, was where I learned the most about myself.

One of my favorite questions to ask clients is one I learned from a mentor: *What is something you are grateful for now that you weren't grateful for at the time?*

I'm grateful for the stroke.

I almost died, and it woke me up to what actually mattered, to my own limiting beliefs about achievement and worthiness, to the changes I needed to make in how I worked and how I lived. I couldn't have seen any of that while I was in it. I certainly wasn't grateful in that ICU bed, or when my knees were bloody from collapsing in a parking lot with numb legs, or when I imagined myself never running again.

But I am grateful now. And not just for the wake-up call. I'm grateful because I'm different. Softer. More curious. Less driven by achievement and more drawn to meaning. Now a recovering Type A workaholic who doesn't take things so seriously anymore.

One of the great mysteries of my life is this: Did my personality change because my psychology changed? Because of how I processed the trauma, the meaning I made of it, the slow work of rehabilitating after a traumatic brain injury? Or did it change because of the wonder of the human brain? Research has shown that the brain can recover from injury by rewiring itself. An injury in the motor cortex can repair by recruiting from other regions entirely. Did my brain, in healing itself, remake who I am?

I'll never know. But I'm forever grateful for it.

That transformation, from crisis to clarity, from suffering to insight, from something you'd never choose to something that remade your life, is what I help others find. Not through advice. Not through someone telling them what to do. Through questions that help them discover their own answers.

If you're reading this, you probably already want to help people grow. But if you're like most well-intentioned managers, mentors, and coaches I've worked with, you're doing more telling than asking. More advising than listening. Seeing the potential in the people you're trying to help, but not seeing them grow into the person you know they could be. And you're likely both frustrated by this.

This book will show you what's actually happening in those conversations, why advice-giving doesn't create lasting change (even when it's good advice), and how to help people think for themselves. Because real transformation doesn't come from being told what to do. It comes from discovering your own answers.

TABLE OF CONTENTS

INTRODUCTION

It is time to evolve the way we help people grow.

Make Them Think is both a rallying cry and a roadmap. It marks a shift away from old habits of telling, advising, and fixing, and toward coaching in a way that helps people think for themselves. It invites you into conversations that spark insight, strengthen ownership, and lead to meaningful action.

It is not only a new method. It is a new mindset.

It teaches you how to stop carrying the burden of having all the answers and how to make people think with clarity and confidence so they can take action toward results that truly last.

The Gap in Modern Coaching

Despite our best intentions, much of what we call coaching today does not create real change. It often takes the form of quick fixes that look good on paper but do not work in practice. It becomes venting without progress. It becomes advice-giving disguised as mentoring, which pressures the advice-giver to always know the right answer and leaves the other person dependent rather than empowered, frustrated that they can't seem to make substantive change.

For many managers, coaches, and mentors, coaching has become nothing more than a plan. It might be a downloadable marathon plan for a first-time runner, a performance plan for an employee who wants to advance, or a sticker chart for a child. But plans rely on willpower and discipline, two cognitive resources that are already strained by the demands of modern life. People try to push through, but they hit walls in motivation, energy, discipline, and confidence. They begin to believe something is wrong with them.

Real growth requires more than a plan. It requires a shift in thinking. Yet most managers and coaches default to prescriptive advice and cheerleading. We tell people what to do, but we rarely help them understand why they are stuck or how their thinking is shaping their behavior.

The world's best coaches have always known that insight precedes action. When we ask better questions and listen with generosity, we help people take ownership of their choices and move toward genuine, lasting change.

What I Have Learned from Coaching Executives and Athletes
I am a certified executive coach (International Coaching Federation, NeuroLeadership Institute) trained in Mindfulness-Based Stress Reduction, and a certified running coach through the Road Runners Club of America. Working in both corporate and athletic environments has taught me one truth above all others:

The most powerful insights come from within.

The coach's job is to guide a creative and thought-provoking conversation that helps someone uncover what is true for them. From there, you lead them from vision to insight to action through questions that expand awareness and reflective listening that strengthens clarity.

Breakthroughs happen when people discover something they did not know they were thinking. Those moments of awareness, whether they feel like an "aha" or an "oh crap," hold the key to real transformation. No amount of advice can replace the ownership that comes when someone sees their situation in a new way and decides how they want to act based on that new insight.

Whether you coach athletes, employees, or a team of any kind, the work is never just about the surface goal. It is about helping people navigate the mental patterns that influence every part of their lives. It is about helping them understand themselves so they can shift the thinking that has been holding them back.

The Same Stories Show Up Everywhere

The stories that limit people in one area of life tend to limit them everywhere. The perfectionism that delays a project also slows progress on a passion. The fear of judgment that keeps someone quiet in meetings also keeps them from expressing their creativity. The inner voice that says "I cannot do this" during a hard workout doesn't stay on the running trail. It follows them into their relationships and work.

When you learn to ask questions that make people think, you help them:

- Distinguish what is true from what is unhelpful mental chatter
- Transform their relationship with uncertainty and discomfort
- Tune into their own inner guidance
- Discover insights that create a ripple effect throughout their life and work

Your Competitive Advantage

Your true advantage as a coach is your ability to create a thought-provoking partnership that goes beyond tactics or advice. When you help people think more clearly and more boldly, they develop ownership of their choices and actions. This is what makes you irreplaceable.

Anyone can offer tips or frameworks. Very few coaches help people see something meaningful about themselves and apply that insight to everything that matters. Very few coaches ask the question that changes someone's direction. Very few leaders create conversations that people remember years later because it was the moment they finally understood what had been holding them back.

What if the most powerful thing you could do as a leader is not to provide answers, but to ask better questions that help people find their own? What could become possible if the people you coach began to think with greater clarity and take action with greater ownership?

A Note on Language

Throughout this book, I use the word "client" to refer to the person you are coaching. If you are a professional coach, this is literal. If you are a manager, a parent, a mentor, or someone who wants to help another person grow, read "client" as shorthand for the person on the other side of the conversation. I also use the word "coach" to describe anyone who facilitates thinking, insight, and action in another person. The principles are the same in every context.

In This Book

- You will learn what neuroscience, psychology, and communication research reveal about how to create the conditions for people to do their best thinking, and how insight leads to ownership and action.
- You will discover four key coaching practices that will help you cultivate presence, curiosity, and the ability to guide transformative conversations.
- You will be introduced to a coaching model that moves people from vision to insight to action with clarity and confidence.
- You will see how to put this model into practice in both hallway conversations and with people you have coached for years.

This book invites you into a new way of thinking and a new way of leading everyday conversations. It will show you how to help people think for themselves, act with ownership, and change their lives in ways that last.

Your Legacy

By applying the methods in this book, you will help people create a life and career that are better than they believed possible. They will achieve their goals and perform better, yes. More importantly, they will remember you as the person who helped them see something they could not see on their own. You will become the coach who asked the question that shifted everything. You will become the leader who believed they had the answers within them long before they believed it themselves.

That is the kind of coach people never forget.

PART I

THE
SCIENCE

What the Behavioral Sciences Teach Us About Unlocking Peak Performance

Information about human behavior is everywhere these days, from academic journals to TikTok. Yet knowing about cognitive biases or neuroplasticity doesn't instinctively make someone a great coach. What sets transformational coaches apart isn't just what they know, but how they think, listen, and show up in service of others.

My coaching philosophy draws from neuroscience, psychology, communication theory, and somatic practices. Not as a collection of techniques to "hack" behavior, but as lenses that deepen my understanding of the whole person. These fields illuminate the questions clients bring to coaching: "Why do I keep sabotaging myself?" "How can two reasonable people completely misunderstand each other?" "What's really stopping me from doing what I say I want to do?"

Great coaches don't just diagnose these challenges. They create the conditions for clients to discover their own answers. They think differently about what drives human behavior, listen deeply enough to hear what's beneath the surface, and lead transformation by trusting the wisdom already present in the people they serve.

Before we dive into the four practices that create the conditions for leading transformation, let's start with the scientific foundation: four principles that explain why these shifts matter.

Four Main Principles

- The brain works by making connections, and every brain is wired differently.
- The brain's primary job is to keep us safe by detecting threats and discovering rewards. Threats always come first.

- The brain has two systems of thinking: one that is intentional and slow, another that is instinctive and automatic.
- Our bodies act as interpreters of the subconscious.

CHAPTER 1

Every Brain is
Wired Differently

L et's do an exercise together. I'll say a word, and you quickly recall the first word, thought, or image that pops into your mind. Ready?

What is the first thing that comes to your mind when I say...

BANANA?

This is my favorite exercise when I teach coaching skills to organizations. Immediately, people start yelling out their answers: bread, monkey, apple (that one always cracks me up), and there's one in every audience who says "banana hammock."

Have you ever wondered why two people can experience the same event and walk away with entirely different understandings? Or why a personal development strategy like "time blocking" works brilliantly for one person but completely fails for another? Or why one person's obvious solution is another person's blind spot?

Neuroscience offers a compelling answer: while we all share the same basic brain architecture (the structures and regions that keep us alive and functioning), the intricate wiring of our neural connections is as unique as a fingerprint.

Genetics provides the blueprint, but experience creates the wiring that guides how we think, feel, and act.

From birth, our brains constantly rewire based on what we encounter, think, and do. This is called neuroplasticity. This means that even identical twins develop distinct neural circuits due to their unique experiences, which is crucial for understanding individual coaching needs.

Neuroplasticity is also why coaching is effective: our brains remain malleable throughout life, capable of forming new connections, adapting to new contexts, and reorganizing in response to insight and practice.

This neural uniqueness explains why we all had different instinctive responses to the word "banana." A parent whose toddler just smashed a banana in their hair that morning, a runner who was offered a banana at the finish line of a race where they beat their personal record, and a jokester who associates a banana with a skimpy men's bathing suit will all have different first associations. Experiences that are emotionally charged, recent, or frequent pop into our mind first.

Understanding that each person's brain has been uniquely wired by their lived experience fundamentally changes how great coaches think, listen, and lead. There is no universal blueprint for human behavior. Only patterns, tendencies, and the remarkable capacity for change.

This is why great coaches never assume they know what's happening inside another person's uniquely wired brain. They never lead with advice based on their own experience, but rather with curiosity, seeking to understand how the person they're talking with is experiencing the situation at hand.

Reflection Questions:

→ What was the first thing that came to mind when you read the word "banana"? Why might that have been the first association that popped into your mind? What cognitive shortcuts or biases of your own might account for that?

→ Think back to a time when you and another person had completely different understandings of the same situation. Maybe you offered advice that worked for you but didn't land for them, or expected them to "get" something that seemed obvious to you. What assumptions were you making about their thinking that, in hindsight, might not have been true for them?

→ Look ahead to an upcoming conversation. How does it feel to consider that the person you're talking with is processing everything through a completely different set of cognitive filters than you are? Does this change how you might approach the conversation?

Now that we understand how uniquely our brains are wired, let's look at what all brains are wired to do: protect us from threat.

CHAPTER 2

Survival Comes First

Here's another question for you. What do you think is the brain's #1 job?

To think? To control the body? To process information? To learn?

All true of the brain, but not its #1 job. The brain's #1 job is to keep us alive.

Our brains are constantly asking one question: is this a threat or a reward? Is this something to move toward or away from? That question runs in the background of every experience. The email that just landed in your inbox. The tone of your manager's voice. The look on your partner's face when they walk through the door. Based on the answer, your brain mobilizes a response. Threat triggers defense. Reward triggers pursuit.

This explains why our behavior shifts so dramatically based on how safe we feel. Threat and reward don't just influence our thinking. They change who we are moment to moment. Throughout this book, I use the term defensive mode to describe times when we're focused on protecting ourselves, and discovery mode to describe those times when we feel safe and open. It won't surprise you to hear that we are far more likely to have a creative, productive conversation when we're in discovery mode than when we're in defensive mode.

Defensive Mode: Moving Away from Threat

Picture this: you're out for a morning run when a cyclist comes around a blind corner, heading straight for you. Before you can even register what's happening, you've already jumped out of its path. Heart pounding, breath short, you stand there marveling at how your body reacted before your mind had a chance to weigh in.

This is your survival system in action. When it detects danger, it doesn't wait for permission. It triggers a fight, flight, or freeze response instantly. In this case, flight saved you. The freeze came a moment later as you stood there wondering what had just happened. And if you shouted a few choice words at the cyclist as they sped off, that was fight joining the party.

This defensive response is a good example of the brain's powerful instinctive system taking control, not just affecting our perception or choices, but driving our immediate actions.

Here's how it works: when a situation feels outside our control, our brain floods our system with stress hormones like adrenaline and cortisol. Our breathing accelerates. Our hearts pound. Our thinking narrows. Everything in our body is saying: handle the threat, now.

This response is driven by a part of the brain called the amygdala. You don't need to remember the name — what matters is what it does. It's constantly scanning for anything uncertain, ambiguous, or new, and it's sensitive enough to react to something as subtle as a frown. All of this happens faster than conscious thought, which is critical when a split second can save us.

This speed is impressive. But it comes at a cost.

First, its speed often comes at the expense of accuracy. Better safe than sorry.

Second, when you feel threatened, your brain shifts resources away from its slower, more sophisticated intentional system. That's useful when there's a physical threat in the room. But when the "danger" is an email with a critical tone that requires a thoughtful response, it's not helpful that you've just taken your strongest thinking offline.

This isn't a design flaw. It's a feature that kept our ancestors alive. The human who heard rustling in the bushes and correctly assumed it was a predator lived to pass on their genes. The one who thought "probably just the wind" did not. Over millennia, our brains evolved to prioritize threat detection over opportunity seeking because the cost of missing a threat was far higher than the cost of missing a reward.

In modern life, we're rarely facing actual predators. But our brains haven't caught up. We still respond to perceived danger with the same wiring that kept our ancestors alive.

And here's the complicating twist: your brain perceives social threats, like criticism or rejection, as just as real as physical danger.

That critical email from your boss? Threat. That awkward silence in a meeting? Threat. The possibility of failure, judgment, or rejection? All threats.

It takes very little to flip us into defensive mode. And once we're there, we're not our most collaborative, creative, or intentional selves. We're in survival mode, not growth mode.

Discovery Mode: Moving Toward Reward
While our defensive system scans for threats, we also have a reward system doing the opposite: looking for things worth pursuing. This includes the obvious rewards like food and rest, but also subtler ones

like connection, recognition, and the satisfaction of doing meaningful work.

When the reward system spots something appealing, it floods us with dopamine and endorphins. These are the neurochemicals behind wanting and liking, and they're powerful motivators. They create an open, curious, forward-looking state of mind. I call this discovery mode.

When we're in discovery mode, we think better. Without the survival system sounding alarms, our intentional system stays fully online. We have access to more mental resources: creativity, flexibility, the ability to hold multiple perspectives at once. Research backs this up: positive mood correlates strongly with the ability to solve complex problems.

Discovery mode isn't about avoiding hard things. It's about approaching them from a state where we can do our best thinking.

The practical question for coaches is: how do you help someone stay in discovery mode when the pull toward defense is so strong? The answer is to focus on what they're moving toward, not what they're running from. When the brain locks onto something rewarding, something worth pursuing, thinking opens rather than contracts. That's where insight becomes possible.

Why This Matters for Coaches
Understanding this discover-defend dynamic changes everything about how we show up in conversation.

First, everything I've just described applies to you too. Coaches can slip into defensive mode just as easily as the people we're coaching. This means we need to manage our own state before and during coaching conversations. If you walk into a session rushed, stressed, or preoccupied, you're more likely to be in defensive mode yourself. And defensive mode is contagious. The person you're coaching will pick up on your tension, and their amygdala will start scanning for what's wrong.

Second, we do everything we can to keep our clients in discovery mode rather than defensive mode. This means paying attention to how we ask questions (curious rather than interrogating), how we respond to what they share (with warmth rather than judgment), and how we create safety in the conversation (so their brain isn't busy protecting them from us). We'll explore specific methods for doing this throughout Part II.

The goal isn't to eliminate all discomfort. Growth often requires some productive tension. But there's a difference between the tension of stretching toward something new and the tension of defending yourself from a threat. Great coaches learn to create the former while minimizing the latter.

Reflection Questions:
→ When was the last time you had an "aha" moment? Where were you? What helped create the conditions for that insight to come to you?
→ Think about a recent moment when you felt yourself shift into defensive mode. What was the trigger? How did your body feel? What happened to your thinking—did you notice yourself becoming more rigid, reactive, or narrow in your perspective?
→ Consider a coaching conversation (or any important conversation) that didn't go well. Looking back, what can you observe about yourself? What was your state going into the conversation? Were you rushing in, stressed, and depleted?

What would you say about the state of the other person? What signals were there that you or they either started or had shifted into defensive mode?

→ When you're about to have a meaningful conversation, what helps you show up as your best?

CHAPTER 3

The Brain Runs Two Systems

O ur brains are remarkable. They keep our hearts beating while simultaneously interpreting the present and predicting the future, protecting us from threats and steering us toward rewards. To manage all of this, the brain runs two very different systems in parallel. Psychologist Daniel Kahneman famously called this "fast" and "slow" thinking. The fast system is instinctive, relying on patterns and shortcuts. The slow system is intentional, handling novel situations and integrating multiple perspectives.

I use "intentional" and "instinctive" rather than Kahneman's "fast" and "slow" because those labels describe what each system offers us, not just how quickly they operate. One isn't better than the other. Both are essential and adaptive. As coaches, our job is to recognize which system is running the show, in ourselves and in our clients, and create the conditions that leverage the strengths of each.

The Intentional System

Let's start with the system we're most aware of: the one behind our conscious, careful thinking. Most of this processing happens in the prefrontal cortex, and it goes by many names in scientific circles: the controlled system, the explicit system, the reflective system.

Kahneman calls it the slow system because it's the slower of the two. I call it the intentional system.

The intentional system handles the thinking we can't do on autopilot: reasoning, self-control, creativity, and forward thinking. It's also the state of mind in which we're most collaborative and open to multiple perspectives, because it's less driven by instinctive perception.

We lean on our intentional system any time we're trying to think through a new situation that isn't habitual. Whether we're helping a stressed loved one, facing a personal challenge, or simply doing something for the first time, we're asking our intentional system to review disparate data points, connect that information to experience, make sense of it all, generate options, and evaluate those options wisely. This process involves logic, certainly, but also creativity, empathy, and receptivity to new perspectives.

The intentional system is also required for self-mastery. It's involved whenever we resist temptation, like when we pick the apple instead of the candy for our afternoon snack, or bite our tongue rather than blurt out a sharp response. This self-control function is central to what scientists call "emotional regulation," the ability to keep our cool when we're upset and to concentrate despite distractions.

Finally, our hardworking intentional system is responsible for planning: creating a vision of the ideal future, setting specific goals, ideating possible strategies, and deciding on next steps. That requires abstract thinking. We must imagine what the future looks like, consider various paths to get there, and assess the eventual benefits of each path. We run these complex calculations every day, even when our goal is just deciding what to have for dinner.

When our intentional system is running the show, we're the version of ourselves we'd like to be all the time: patient, creative, collaborative, and wise.

But of course, that's not how we operate all the time.

The Instinctive System

So how do we handle the nonstop cacophony of information that defines modern life? The answer lies in the brain's second system, which I call the instinctive system. Like the intentional system, it goes by many names in the research: the automatic system, the implicit system, the intuitive mind. You might know it as the subconscious. Kahneman calls it the "fast" system, since it operates so much more quickly than the sophisticated but slower conscious mind.

By whatever name, this system's magic is automation. Its quick, instinctive processes remove the need for us to think consciously about every little thing we do. This lets our intentional system focus on what requires conscious attention: novel problems, difficult choices, and long-term planning.

The instinctive system lightens the load on our intentional system in several ways. The most obvious is how it handles familiar tasks by turning them into autopilot routines. Think of everything you do on autopilot: the walk from the subway to your office, the way your fingers find the right keys when you type. These aren't simple actions, but repetition has made them automatic.

The instinctive system also acts as a filter. It rapidly sorts through incoming information, flags what seems relevant, and discards the rest before it ever reaches conscious awareness. This is why you don't notice every sound in a crowded room or every car on a busy street. Your instinctive system has already decided what's worth your attention, reducing the load on your intentional system.

The instinctive system isn't inferior to the intentional system; it's just different. It holds the accumulated wisdom of every experience we've ever had, processed and stored below conscious awareness. When we get a "gut feeling" about a person or situation, that's our instinctive system pattern-matching against thousands of past experiences faster than our conscious mind could ever analyze. These signals are worth attending to. The goal isn't to override our instincts but to bring them into conversation with our intentional thinking.

How the Instinctive System Takes Shortcuts
Speed requires trade-offs. The instinctive system moves fast because it simplifies. Psychologists have identified hundreds of these shortcuts, which they call heuristics, and given them labels you might recognize, such as confirmation bias, recency bias, frequency bias, and so on. What all of these have in common is this: they direct our intentional system's conscious attention toward things that feel comparatively easy to wrap our brains around, while deprioritizing anything that feels harder to grasp.

This gives rise to the truth behind the popular saying "We don't experience the world as it is, we experience it as we are." We are constantly experiencing an edited, simplified version of reality.

Why This Matters for Coaches
Great coaches appreciate the strengths of both systems and recognize when each is running the show in themselves and in their clients.

When someone says, "I don't know why I keep doing this," or "I know what I should do, but I just can't seem to do it," they're experiencing the tension between these two systems. The instinctive system is running the show, while the intentional system watches helplessly from the sidelines. When a client tells you, "I know I shouldn't micromanage my team, but I can't seem to stop," their intentional system sees the problem clearly. But their instinctive system keeps running the old pattern.

Our job as coaches isn't to shame people for their instinctive responses or to simply tell them to "try harder" with their intentional system. But it's also not to help clients silence their instincts and operate purely from intention. That would ignore the vast majority of what the brain knows. Instead, we help clients notice what their gut is telling them, surface it, and examine it alongside their conscious reasoning. The best coaching happens when both systems are in dialogue.

Our job is to help clients become aware of which system is driving their behavior and to create the conditions where their intentional system can show up and lead, informed by their instinctive wisdom rather than in opposition to it.

The chapters that follow will show you how.

Reflection Questions
→ What instinctive patterns show up most often in your coaching (or management, or in relationships)? What are your automatic responses to specific situations, like jumping in with advice, getting defensive when challenged, or making assumptions about what someone needs?
→ When you first read about the two systems of thinking, did you find yourself labeling one as "good" and the other as "bad"? What would you say now about the strengths of both systems?
→ Think about your daily routine. What parts happen on auto-pilot, instinctively, without you having to think about them?

When does your instinctive system serve you brilliantly, and when does it get in your way? Are there patterns or shortcuts that used to work but no longer do?

→ Where in your life is there something you know you want to do, but you just can't seem to do it? What might your instinctive system be protecting or preserving? What might help your intentional system show up?

CHAPTER 4

The Body Talks

A t some level, we all know that the mind and body are connected. You know that worry can feel like tightness in your chest, a bad night's sleep makes you short-tempered, and something as small as a blister on your heel can distract your attention away from everything else.

So it's strange that most coaching frameworks act as if the body doesn't exist. They focus exclusively on the thinking mind: intellect, knowledge, and cognitive strategies. They operate above the water-line of conscious awareness, addressing only the thoughts we can readily identify and articulate.

Here's what traditional coaching misses: the vast majority of what drives our behavior operates below the level of conscious awareness. When you coach only the conscious mind, you're not seeing the whole picture.

The Subconscious and Conscious Meet in the Body

The body is where we can access what's happening beneath the surface. Thoughts, emotions, and past experiences (including stress and trauma) shape our physical sensations and behavioral patterns in ways our conscious thinking can't always access or explain.

You walk into a room for a presentation and immediately feel your stomach tighten. You're in a conversation with a colleague and notice your jaw clenching. You're making a decision and feel a subtle expansion in your chest when you land on the correct answer. These aren't random physical events. Your body is communicating information your conscious mind hasn't yet processed.

Body awareness is both a practical skill and a philosophical shift. When you bring it into coaching, you're recognizing that the wisdom clients seek isn't only in their heads. It's already present in their physical experience, waiting to be noticed.

What Body-Centered Coaching Looks Like

A body-centered approach to coaching helps individuals foster self-awareness and create lasting change by recognizing the connection between mind and body. It emphasizes being fully present in the moment and cultivating a "felt sense" of the body's signals (tension, ease, heat, constriction, expansion) to tap into wisdom that lives below conscious thought.

This approach also helps clients understand and regulate their nervous system. Remember our earlier discussion of defensive mode versus discovery mode? Many clients are stuck in a chronic fight, flight, or freeze response due to ongoing stress. Their bodies are sending constant alarm signals that their conscious minds may not even register. By bringing awareness to these physical patterns, coaches can help clients build resilience and emotional balance at a physiological level, not just a cognitive one, making change more sustainable.

The goal is to move beyond intellectual understanding to embodied action. It's the difference between knowing you should set boundaries and actually feeling in your stomach when a boundary has been crossed. It's the difference between understanding logically that you're burned out and sensing the heaviness in your limbs that's been trying to tell you to rest for weeks.

The Cost of Ignoring the Body

You ask thoughtful questions. You listen carefully. Your client says all the right things. They understand the issue. They know what they need to do. And yet something feels off. You sense something beneath the surface but don't have the tools to access it.

So you work harder. You ask more questions. You try to think your way through a problem that thinking alone can't solve.

Here's what's happening: you're coaching the conscious mind while the subconscious runs the show.

Bringing the Body Into the Coaching Conversation

When you coach with both body and mind in awareness, you're no longer limited to what clients can readily put into words. You gain access to signals that reveal what's actually going on and what's ready to shift, even if clients find it challenging to notice or describe their physical experiences at first.

This doesn't mean you need to become a somatic therapist or a bodyworker. It means learning to ask different questions and make different observations.

"What are you noticing in your body right now as you talk about this?"

"When you imagine taking that action, what physical sensations come up?"

"I noticed that you looked down as you said that. What's happening there?"

It means learning to notice when a client's body language contradicts their words. When they say "I'm excited about this opportunity," but their shoulders slump and voice flattens, that's worth exploring. Naming what you see helps clients learn to trust what their bodies are telling them.

It means helping clients understand that their nervous system's fight, flight, or freeze response isn't just a mental state. It's a full-body experience that shapes their perception, narrows their thinking, and drives their behavior.

And it means recognizing that the path to lasting change isn't just about insight and action planning. It's about helping clients identify, understand, and work with the physical patterns that have been running the show all along.

When you coach this way, you're finally working with the whole person. You're accessing the vast territory that lives below the waterline of conscious awareness. And that's where the fundamental transformation happens.

Reflection Questions

→ Think about a challenging situation you're facing in your own life. What physical sensations show up in your body when you think about this situation? Try naming the bodily sensation itself ("constriction in the chest," "a sinking feeling in my stomach," "tightness in my jaw") rather than attaching meaning or emotional labels to it. Practice relating physical sensations to information, just like you would with any other data.

→ Think of the last time you felt a "hell yes" response rush through your body. What did that feel like in the physical sense? What words or emotions do you associate with that physical feeling?

→ Pause right now and scan your body. What physical sensations are you noticing? Are there areas that feel tense or constricted? Areas of ease? Warmth or coolness? Just notice without judgment. This is your body speaking.

→ Recall a time when someone's words didn't match their physical demeanor. What felt off to you? What cues were you picking up in their posture, voice, breathing, or energy? How might you approach a similar situation in the future with curiosity?

PART II

THE
PRACTICE

So what does all this science mean for you?

Whether you're a professional coach, a manager, a parent, or just someone who wants to bring out the best in the people you care about, everything we've covered so far matters in every conversation you have.

Think about it. Every coaching conversation involves someone whose brain has been uniquely wired by their lived experience. Someone whose nervous system is constantly scanning for threats or rewards, and is at any given time more likely to be in defensive mode than discovery mode. Someone with two systems of thinking: one that's fast, instinctive, and automatic, and another that's slow, intentional, and deliberate. And someone who can only consciously access a fraction of the thoughts, feelings, and reactions flooding their system at any moment.

That's a lot happening beneath the surface. And it's all happening within you simultaneously.

You're probably doing a lot of things right. You're asking questions. You're giving your full attention. You genuinely care about helping. But somehow the conversations stay surface-level. Your client nods along, agrees with the plan, and then nothing really shifts. You leave the session wondering what you missed.

The question becomes: How do you actually coach in a way that honors the reality of two human beings having a human interaction? How do you create the conditions for someone to access their intentional system when their instinctive patterns keep taking over? How do you help them stay in discovery mode when their nervous system is primed to flip into defense at the slightest hint of threat?

What Gets in the Way

Well-intentioned coaching goes sideways when we move too quickly, trying to fix, reassure, or prove our value. It's not malicious. In fact, it usually comes from a genuine desire to help. But it's driven by our own instincts and urgency rather than by what the client actually needs.

When this happens, we react to what's said rather than listening for what's underneath. We view the client through the lens of our own lived experience, automatic perceptions, and biases. We inadvertently make them feel judged or misunderstood, which flips them straight into defensive mode. We tell more than we ask. We focus on the problem instead of the solution. We hear the words but miss the patterns. We repeat back what someone said instead of reflecting on what we observe.

The result? The client's automatic thinking stays in control. Their defenses remain up. And real insight, ownership, and the right actions to take never have a chance to emerge.

What Creates the Conditions for Insight, Ownership, and Real Change

Effective coaching is spacious. It's grounded in curiosity, awareness, and presence. It starts with unconditional positive regard: a fundamental trust in the client's inner wisdom and a commitment to creating psychological safety where insight can emerge from within.

When you coach this way, you regard the client as resourceful and whole. You recognize that your job isn't to have all the answers but to create the conditions where their answers can surface. You're asking far more than you're telling (about 90/10 is the right ratio). You're keeping the conversation focused on solutions rather than spiraling into problem analysis. And you're listening generously: observing beneath surface-level responses to identify underlying patterns, energy shifts, and belief systems, then contributing observations that open new perspectives.

The Shift Starts With You

Here's what makes this challenging: the shift from ineffective to effective coaching is as much about how you manage yourself as it is about how you lead the conversation. Recognize your own instinctive patterns and biases, and develop awareness of how they influence your responses, so you can stay present and create the right conditions for insight.

When you rush into a coaching conversation depleted and stressed, you bring your own activated nervous system into the room. When you're operating from your instinctive system (defaulting to familiar patterns and shortcuts), you're not fully present to what's emerging. Managing your nervous system helps you stay calm and confident, creating a safe space for your client to explore and grow.

The Four Shifts

The chapters that follow introduce four fundamental shifts. These aren't random techniques you add to your toolkit. They're deliberate practices designed to work with the realities of having a human body and brain rather than against them.

Shift 1: Regard The Client as Resourceful and Whole. Your stance toward the client creates psychological safety. Trust their inner wisdom and lived experience. Recognize that they likely see things entirely differently from you, and their knowledge is just as valid.

Shift 2: Ask, Don't Tell. Aim for a 90/10 ratio of asking to telling. You're asking because you want to understand how they see the situation, what's ideal for them, how they might want to move forward, and what they want to learn. It's about their thinking, not yours. This creates the conditions for them to take ownership, tap into their own inner motivation, and make changes that actually matter to them.

Shift 3: Focus on Solutions, Not Problems. When you dwell on problems, you keep the client focused on what's wrong. Their defensive system stays activated, their thinking narrows, and they spiral deeper into the problem's details and drama without moving forward. It's inefficient and ineffective. When you focus on solutions, you shift their attention toward possibility. What do they actually want? What would "better" look like? This puts them in discovery mode as they imagine potential rewards from this new way of doing things. It's a more creative, receptive, and collaborative state of mind.

Shift 4: Listen Generously. Most of us listen just well enough to respond. Generous listening goes deeper. You're observing beneath the surface: noticing patterns, energy shifts, and what's not being said. You're paying attention when the body contradicts the words. And when you speak, you contribute observations that open new perspectives and move the conversation forward, not simply repeating what you heard. This is how you access what words alone can't reveal.

Together, these shifts create conditions that help both you and your client stay in discovery mode. They engage the intentional system's capacity for creativity and insight. They tap into the body's wisdom and the patterns operating beneath conscious awareness. And they're rooted in the belief that the client already possesses the wisdom they're seeking. They just need the right environment to access it.

Master these shifts, and it changes not just your coaching conversations but every relationship that matters to you.

Reflection Questions

→ Think about a recent interaction in which you were trying to help someone. Were you helping them think, or were you doing the thinking for them? What percentage of the time were you asking versus telling?

→ Think of a conversation that felt particularly effective. What conditions did you create that allowed insight to emerge? How were you showing up differently than usual? How were you regarding the other person at that moment?

→ Consider an upcoming conversation with someone whose perspective or approach differs significantly from yours. What assumptions or beliefs are you bringing that might not be true for them? What would it look like to regard this person as resourceful and whole, even if they see things differently than you do?

CHAPTER 5

Regard The Client as Resourceful and Whole

The Concept

Unconditional positive regard is the core principle that underpins effective coaching. Clarifying this first shift is essential because it defines your identity as a coach and sets the stage for all other shifts. Get this wrong, and nothing else works.

Coined by psychologist Carl Rogers, unconditional positive regard describes an attitude of complete acceptance: viewing the client as fundamentally capable, whole, and possessing their own inner wisdom, regardless of their current struggles or choices.

This doesn't mean you approve of everything they do or agree with every decision. It means you trust that they are doing the best they can with the resources they currently have, and that the answers they're seeking already exist within them. Your job isn't to fix them, save them, or show them the "right" way. Your job is to create psychological safety where their own insights can emerge.

When you hold unconditional positive regard, you're communicating something profound: "I see you as capable. I trust your process. I believe in your ability to figure this out." This stance fosters trust and safety, making your clients feel truly supported, respected, and confident in your presence.

The Science Behind It

Remember the brain's central organizing principle? Every moment, your client's nervous system is asking: "Is this a threat or a reward?" When someone feels judged, questioned, or "wrong," their brain registers a social threat. Naomi Eisenberger's research shows that social threats activate neural pathways similar to those activated by physical pain, highlighting why unconditional positive regard is vital for safety and trust.

If you're reading this book, you have every intention of creating a safe space for people to be completely themselves. But remember that your client's brain is constantly scanning for any potential sign of risk. When they sense judgment, even subtle, their amygdala fires, their intentional system goes offline, and they shift into defensive mode. They're no longer able to access creativity, consider multiple perspectives, or generate insights. They're protecting themselves from the perceived threat of your disapproval.

When you approach them with unconditional positive regard, you create the opposite effect. Their nervous system registers safety. They stay in discovery mode, where they can access their intentional system's capacity for reasoning, self-reflection, and insight.

Remember that each brain is uniquely wired by lived experience. When you filter what your client says through your own biases, you're imposing your wiring on theirs. You might think "I would never feel that way" or "that's not how I would handle it." But your way isn't their way. Your wiring isn't their wiring. When you unconsciously hold them to your standards of how they "should" think, feel, or act, you break the psychological safety that makes growth possible.

Why This Is Hard

Let's be honest: unconditional positive regard is one of the hardest shifts to master because it requires overriding automatic judgments and comparisons rooted in deeply ingrained instincts.

First, your instinctive system is constantly comparing the client's experience to your own. When they describe a situation, your brain automatically references similar situations from your memory, complete with the judgments and conclusions you drew from those experiences. "If I were in that situation, I would..." is running in the background, whether you say it out loud or not.

Second, when you see someone struggling, your brain's reward system wants to help. This often translates into fixing, rescuing, or proving your value by having the answer. This impulse comes from a good place, but it's usually driven by your own need to feel useful rather than what the client actually needs.

Unconditional positive regard is especially challenging when you disagree with a client's choices. Use specific language such as "I hear your perspective, and I trust your process" or "Thank you for sharing that" to stay rooted in your intentional system and uphold safety despite differences. These phrases reinforce acceptance and support which keeps exploration possible.

Finally, our culture has conditioned us to believe that good coaching means having expertise and sharing wisdom. Sitting back and trusting someone else's process can feel passive, even irresponsible. It triggers our own insecurity: "Am I even helping? What's the point of me being here if I'm not telling them what to do?"

Coaching Without Unconditional Positive Regard

The Scenario: Maya is a marketing director considering whether to pursue a VP promotion that would require relocating her family across the country.

Coach: "So you're thinking about the VP role. That's exciting! I actually faced a similar decision five years ago. Here's what I learned: career growth is absolutely worth it, even though the transition is hard at first. Have you thought about what schools you'd want for your kids?"

Maya: "Well, I'm not sure I even want it. The role seems like it might not be the right fit for—"

Coach: "Oh, don't sell yourself short! You're definitely ready for this. You're just scared of the change, which is totally normal. But you can't let fear hold you back from a great opportunity. What specifically are you worried about?"

Maya: "It's not really fear. It's more that the role focuses on metrics and optimization, and what I love about marketing is the creative strategy side—"

Coach: "Right, but at the VP level, you have to focus on business outcomes. That's just part of leadership. You'll still have creative people on your team doing that work. Trust me, once you're in the role, you'll adjust."

What's happening here: The coach has filtered Maya's situation entirely through their own experience and values. They've decided what Maya's problem is (fear of change), what she should value (career advancement over personal preferences), and what the "right" answer is (take the promotion). Maya's nervous system is picking up on the judgment, the subtle message that her hesitation is wrong, that she's "selling herself short." Notice how she keeps trying to share her genuine concern (the nature of the work itself), but the coach keeps redirecting her back to what the coach thinks matters. Maya is likely feeling defensive, misunderstood, and less safe to explore her true feelings.

Coaching With Unconditional Positive Regard
The Scenario: The same situation with Maya.

Coach: "Tell me about the VP role. What's drawing you toward it, and what's giving you pause?"

Maya: "The title and compensation are incredible. It's everything I thought I wanted. But the role focuses heavily on metrics and optimization, and what I love about marketing is the creative strategy side. I know that sounds silly."

Coach: "It doesn't sound silly at all. It sounds like you're paying attention to something important. Say more about that."

Maya: "Everyone keeps congratulating me, asking when I'm going to accept. My husband thinks I'm crazy for even hesitating. Part of me wonders if I'm just being difficult or self-sabotaging."

Coach: "I hear you questioning yourself. And I'm curious: what if there's nothing wrong with you? What if this hesitation is actually wisdom trying to get your attention?"

Maya: "I hadn't thought of it that way."

Coach: "What are you noticing in your body right now as we talk about this?"

Maya: "When I think about everyone's expectations, my chest gets tight. But when you said 'wisdom trying to get your attention,' something relaxed."

Coach: "You're not broken. Not even a little bit. You're someone who's listening to competing pieces of information: what you thought you wanted, what others want for you, and what your body is telling you about the actual work. That's not self-sabotage. That's discernment. What does your body tell you when you imagine yourself in that VP role day-to-day?"

Maya: "Honestly? Heavy. Like I'm wearing a coat that doesn't fit right. The creative strategy work, though? I feel alive just talking about it."

Coach: "I trust that. What does your body know here?"

Maya: "That I've been chasing external validation instead of what actually matters to me."

Coach: "That takes real courage to admit. What becomes possible now that you're being honest about this?"

What's happening here: The coach explicitly validates Maya's experience multiple times, especially when she's judging herself. Notice phrases like "It doesn't sound silly at all," "What if there's nothing wrong with you?" and "You're not broken. Not even a little bit." The coach reframes Maya's hesitation as wisdom and discernment rather than a flaw. When Maya admits something vulnerable, the coach honors that courage rather than glossing over it. Throughout, the coach trusts Maya's experience as valid and real, even when it conflicts with external expectations.

What This Sounds Like in Practice

When you're practicing unconditional positive regard, you'll find yourself saying things like:

- "There's nothing you could tell me that would make me think less of you or doubt your capability."
- "You're not broken for feeling that way. That sounds like a very human reaction."
- "Is there any part of you that feels differently? Let's give that voice a chance to speak."

- "What if the way you're experiencing this is completely valid, even if it's different from how others might experience it?"
- "I trust what you're sensing, even if you can't fully articulate it yet."
- "You're the expert on your own experience. Help me understand what this is like for you."
- "That takes real courage to name."
- "What you're feeling makes complete sense, even if it doesn't match what you think you 'should' feel."

Notice what these phrases do: they explicitly counter self-judgment, validate the client's experience as real and vital, and communicate trust in their inner wisdom, especially in moments when the client might be doubting themselves.

Watch-Outs

You'll know you've lost unconditional positive regard when you notice yourself:

- Thinking "I would never..." or "They should just..."
- Feeling frustrated that they're not "getting it."
- Comparing their situation to your own experience
- Experiencing a tight, contracted feeling in your own body (often a sign that you're regarding their progress as evidence of your performance as a coach)
- Using phrases like "Have you considered..." as a way to sneak in advice rather than genuine curiosity
- Feeling responsible for solving their problem rather than trusting their process
- Getting attached to a particular outcome for them

When you notice these warning signs, pause. Take a breath. Reconnect with the belief that this person is resourceful and whole.

Ask yourself: "What am I making this mean about me?" Often, our judgment of others is actually anxiety about our own value as a coach.

Reflection Questions

→ Think of someone in your life whose choices you struggle to understand or agree with. What automatic judgments or assumptions do you notice yourself making about them? What would it feel like to regard them as resourceful and whole, even while they're making choices you wouldn't make?

→ Recall a time when you felt entirely accepted by another person, even while talking about something hard. How did that feel in your body? What did it make possible for you?

→ Consider an essential upcoming conversation. What biases, assumptions, or comparisons to your own experience might you be bringing into the room? How might those interfere with your ability to see the client clearly? What would you need to do to set those aside?

CHAPTER 6

Ask, Don't Tell

The Concept

Remember the banana exercise from Part I? When I asked, "What's the first thing that comes to mind when I say banana?" When I do this in groups, some people yell out "bread." Others think of monkeys. Runners and running coaches tend to say "finish line," "potassium," or "carbs." My husband would say "BLECH."

Now, imagine you come to me with a problem. "I'm struggling with bananas."

If I immediately jump in and say, "Oh, I have the perfect banana bread recipe!" there's a good chance I've just wasted both our time and started our conversation off on the wrong foot. Why? Because you weren't looking for a banana bread recipe. Maybe you hate the taste of bananas, but your doctor told you to eat more potassium. Perhaps you want to have a banana with you at the starting corral of your next race, but by the time you've taken the subway, they always end up bruised. Maybe your toddler keeps smashing bananas in their hair.

My banana solution only works if we share the same banana problem. And given that every brain has been uniquely wired by lived experience, the chances that we're experiencing the same situation in the same way are remarkably low.

This is of course a silly example, but it illustrates an important point. Great coaches ask far more than they tell. The ratio should be about 90% asking, 10% telling. And that 10% isn't advice. It's clarifying observations and reflections we'll discuss in Chapter 8.

When you ask instead of tell, you're doing something profound: you're centering the conversation around the client's reality (how they see the world, themselves, and the situation) rather than imposing your reality onto theirs.

The Science Behind It
Remember that every brain is wired differently based on lived experience, creating different shortcuts, biases, and ways of processing information. When you tell someone what to do based on your experience, you're assuming your neural wiring maps onto theirs. It doesn't.

But there's an even more critical neurological reality at play: being told what to do can trigger defensive mode.

When you tell someone what they should do, their brain may perceive it as a social threat. A subtle signal that they're not capable of figuring it out themselves, that they're doing it wrong, or that their way of seeing the situation is being dismissed. Their intentional system goes offline. They are no longer in a state where they can access creativity, insight, or their own problem-solving capabilities.

When you ask questions, something different happens. Questions signal: "I trust you to think this through. Your perspective matters. You're capable." This keeps them in discovery mode, where they can actually think.

Here's what else matters: when people discover their own answers, the insights stick. Neuroscience research on memory and learning shows that self-generated insights create stronger neural pathways than information received passively. When you tell someone what to do, they might understand it intellectually. But when they discover it themselves through questioning, it becomes more deeply integrated into their neural circuitry.

Why This Is Hard

The impulse to tell instead of ask runs deep. Here's why this shift is particularly challenging:

First, telling is faster (or so it seems). When you see the solution clearly, it feels inefficient to ask questions and wait for the client to arrive at what you already know. Your instinctive system wants to shortcut the process: "Just do what I already know works."

Second, telling feels like helping. We've been culturally conditioned to believe that having answers demonstrates competence and value. Asking questions can feel like you're not contributing, not earning your keep. It triggers that voice that whispers, "They're paying me for answers, not more questions."

Third, your brain genuinely believes your solution will work for them. This is the curse of the "banana bread" problem. You solved your banana problem with banana bread, and your brain has automatically filed banana bread as "the solution to banana problems." It takes conscious effort to override this and recognize that their banana problem might be completely different from yours.

Fourth, holding back advice requires staying in your intentional system. When someone brings you a problem you've solved before, your instinctive system immediately surfaces your solution and wants to share it. Pausing, asking questions instead, and trusting their process requires you to remain in that slower, more effortful intentional mode.

Finally, some people really do want you to tell them what to do (or at least they really think they do). "Just tell me what to do" is a common request, especially from clients who are overwhelmed or looking for a quick fix. Resisting this invitation and redirecting back to questions takes courage and conviction.

That said, the 90/10 rule isn't dogma. There's a difference between someone asking for a shortcut and someone who is genuinely stuck. If you've tried asking questions a few different ways and they're still coming up empty, silent, or visibly frustrated, holding rigidly to questions can start to feel like withholding. In those moments, you may need to offer a life-raft.

When this happens, I ask permission first. This keeps them in the driver's seat and preserves their sense of autonomy. I'll say something like, "Would you like me to share some examples of how I've seen other people handle this situation? You can see if any resonate with you."

Then I offer three or four short examples of what I've seen work for others. I might include what works for me, but I never offer only my approach. By giving several options, I'm inviting them to notice which one perks their ears up rather than handing them one-dimensional advice. They're still choosing. They're still discovering what works for them.

This is your 10%, used wisely.

Coaching by Telling, not Asking

The Scenario: Marcus is a sales manager struggling with one of his team members, Jamie, who misses deadlines and seems disengaged. Marcus wants coaching on how to handle the situation.

Coach: "Oh, I've dealt with this exact situation before. Here's what you need to do: Set up a performance improvement plan. Document everything. Give Jamie specific metrics to hit and a timeline. Usually, 30 days works well. If they don't meet the metrics, you'll have everything you need to let them go."

Marcus: "I mean, I don't really want to fire Jamie. They've been with the company for years, and when they're on, they're one of my best—"

Coach: "Right, but you can't let poor performance slide. It's not fair to your other team members who are carrying their weight. You need to have a direct conversation about accountability. Here's a script I use: 'I've noticed you've missed the last three deadlines. This isn't acceptable, and here's what needs to change.'"

Marcus: "The thing is, Jamie hasn't always been like this. Something changed about six months ago, and I'm not sure what—"

Coach: "Look, it doesn't really matter what changed. You're not their therapist. You're their manager. Your job is to set clear expectations and hold people accountable. I learned this the hard way: when you're too soft on underperformers, you lose your top performers. Just trust me on this."

Marcus: [Shoulders slumping] "Yeah, you're probably right."

What's happening here: The coach is telling Marcus what to do based on their own experience and assumptions, without understanding Marcus's actual situation, his relationship with Jamie, his leadership values, or what might be driving Jamie's behavior change. Notice how every time Marcus tries to share context, the coach redirects him back to their pre-packaged solution. Marcus's language shifts from engaged exploration ("when they're on, they're one of my best") to resigned compliance ("Yeah, you're probably right"). The coach has centered the conversation around their own reality, not Marcus's. And crucially, Marcus hasn't discovered anything. He has a prescription but no ownership, no insight, and likely no motivation to implement it.

Coaching by Asking, not Telling
The Scenario: The same situation with Marcus.

Coach: "Tell me about Jamie. What's going on?"

Marcus: "They're missing deadlines and seem totally disengaged. It's affecting the whole team."

Coach: "When you say 'disengaged,' what are you noticing specifically?"

Marcus: "They're quiet in meetings. They used to contribute ideas and ask questions. Now they just sit there. And the deadline thing. They used to be so reliable."

Coach: "You said 'used to.' When did you notice the shift?"

Marcus: [Pausing] "Maybe six months ago? Actually, now that I think about it, it was right after we reorganized and gave them that new account portfolio."

Coach: "What changed with that new portfolio?"

Marcus: "We thought it was a promotion. Bigger accounts, more responsibility. But..." [long pause] "...I'm realizing now, Jamie loved the creative problem-solving with our smaller clients. The new accounts are more administrative, more process-driven."

Coach: "What does that tell you?"

Marcus: "That maybe I've put my best creative problem-solver into a role that plays to their weaknesses, not their strengths. God, I might have accidentally demoralized them."

Coach: "What do you think Jamie needs to thrive?"

Marcus: "Creative challenges. Client variety. They need to feel like they're solving interesting problems, not just managing processes."

Coach: "So what might be possible here?"

Marcus: [Leaning forward] "I could talk to Jamie about the portfolio. See if there is a way to restructure. Maybe bring in some of the creative work they loved. Or at least understand what's happening for them before I jump to performance management."

Coach: "When will you have that conversation?"

Marcus: "This week. I'm going to ask them what's been happening, what they need. I should have done that six months ago."

What's happening here: The coach asked questions that helped Marcus discover his own insight about what's really going on. Notice the coach never said, "Have you considered that Jamie might be in the wrong role?" or "You should talk to Jamie." Instead, through questions, Marcus arrived at that conclusion himself. The questions guided him from the surface problem (missed deadlines) to the underlying issue (misalignment between Jamie's strengths and their current role) to his own solution (to have a conversation and restructure if needed). Marcus owns this insight. He discovered it. And he's motivated to act on it because it's his answer, not the coach's prescription.

What This Sounds Like in Practice

When you're practicing the 90/10 rule, you'll find yourself asking questions like:

To understand their reality:
- "What's important to you about this?"
- "When you think about this situation, what comes up for you?"
- "How are you experiencing this?"
- "What does that mean to you?"

To deepen exploration:
- "Say more about that."
- "What else?"
- "Tell me more."
- "What's underneath that?"

To generate insight:
- "What does that tell you?"
- "What are you noticing?"
- "If you did know, what would it be?"
- "What would you tell your best friend in this situation?"

To move toward action:
- "What's possible here?"
- "What do you want to be different?"
- "What's one step forward?"
- "When will you do that?"

To check assumptions:
- "Help me understand..."
- "It sounds like …. Am I hearing that right?"
- "What's true for you about this?"

Notice what these questions do: they invite exploration, honor the client's expertise about their own life, and create space for self-discovery. They don't lead the client toward the coach's predetermined answer.

Watch-Outs

You'll know you've slipped into telling mode when you notice yourself:

- Starting sentences with: "You should..." "Have you tried..." "What worked for me was..." "If I were you..."
- Feeling an urgency to give them the answer because you can see it so clearly
- Getting frustrated or impatient when they don't arrive at the conclusion you think is obvious
- Offering advice disguised as questions: "Have you considered _____?" or "What do you think about _____?"
- Talking more than the client in the coaching session
- Feeling satisfied with yourself for having "helped" by telling them what to do
- Noticing the client becoming passive, waiting for you to tell them what to do next

When you catch yourself in telling mode, pause and ask yourself: "What question would help them discover this for themselves?" Then ask that question.

Reflection Questions

→ Track your ratio this week. In your subsequent three coaching conversations (or meaningful conversations of any kind), pay attention to how much you're asking versus telling. What percentage of your talking is questions versus statements, advice, or sharing your own experience? Are you close to 90/10?

→ Notice your impulse to tell. When you feel the urge to give advice or share what worked for you, pause. What are you assuming about the other person's situation? What might be different about their "banana problem" compared to yours?

→ Experiment with questions. The next time someone asks you, "What should I do?" resist the urge to answer directly. Instead, try: "What have you already considered?" or "What does your gut tell you?" Notice what happens when you redirect them back to their own thinking.

→ Think of a time when someone gave you advice that didn't land. How did it feel? Did their solution fit your actual problem? Did you implement it? Now think of a time when someone asked you good questions, and you discovered your own answer. What was different about that experience?

CHAPTER 7

Focus on Solutions, Not Problems

The Concept

Have you ever had a tense conversation with someone, and then hours later you're in the shower or at the gym, and the *perfect* thing to have said just pops into your mind out of nowhere? If so, you've experienced this next point: you cannot solve a problem while focused on the problem. Why? Because when you're focused on a problem, your brain perceives threat, which activates defensive mode and blocks creative problem-solving.

And yet, when someone says, "My coworker is pissing me off," what's your immediate response?

If you're like most humans, you instinctively say: "What happened?"

Workout felt too challenging? "What happened?" Frustrated with someone? "What happened?" Missed a deadline? "What happened?"

It's the most natural, automatic response in the world. It feels compassionate and helpful. After all, how can you help if you don't understand what's wrong?

Here's the problem: "What happened?" is one of the worst questions you can ask if you're actually trying to help someone move forward.

Why? Because "What happened?" will lead you both into at least ten minutes of detail and drama about the problem. Your client will recount every frustrating moment, every person who made things worse, every reason they couldn't succeed.

Meanwhile, you're nodding along, taking notes, feeling like you're being a good coach by "really understanding the situation." But you've just wasted ten minutes that could have been spent actually moving forward.

The way out isn't deeper into the problem. It's toward the solution. Imagining an ideal future state feels rewarding and exciting. It enables us to be more creative, open, and collaborative.

The Better Question: "What's Ideal?"
Instead of "What happened?" try asking: "What's ideal?" or "What do you want instead?"

Consider what happens when you redirect from the problem to the desired outcome:

- "So and so is driving me crazy." → "What is it that you want so and so to do?"
- "My workout felt like crap." → "When you finish a workout feeling great, what's different?"
- "I keep missing deadlines." → "What are the most important deadlines to hit right now?"

These questions do something remarkable: they orient the brain toward possibility instead of threat. They activate the reward system instead of the defensive response. They keep your client in discovery mode, activating their creativity and opening the door to new solutions and insights.

Solution-focused coaching isn't about ignoring problems or pretending struggles don't exist. It's about helping your client imagine a better future for themselves, which keeps them in discovery mode where they can actually find a path forward.

The Science Behind It

Remember the discover-defend spectrum? When you ask someone to recount failures and analyze obstacles, you're systematically activating their threat response. Their brain doesn't distinguish between "I'm reflecting on a problem in a coaching conversation" and "I'm in actual danger." To the amygdala, reliving failure or conflict feels like encountering a predator.

Research published in the *Journal of Positive Psychology* confirms what neuroscience predicts: participants in solution-focused coaching experienced significantly more positive emotions, fewer negative emotions, and higher goal orientation than those in problem-focused coaching. The mechanism is clear. When clients imagine a better future, they stay in discovery mode, where creativity and insight are readily available.

When you ask solution-focused questions, something shifts visibly: shoulders open, gaze lifts, breathing deepens. This isn't just "feeling better." This is the nervous system downregulating, the prefrontal cortex coming back online. Now they have the full power of their executive function, creativity, collaborative thinking, and ability to look at the situation from different perspectives.

But the benefits extend beyond immediate feelings of good. Solution-focused questions activate approach motivation instead of threat avoidance. They strengthen neural pathways associated with capability by helping clients recognize their own past successes. They build self-efficacy and generate momentum through small wins and forward movement.

As Albert Einstein famously said, "You cannot solve a problem with the same mind that created it."

Why This Is Hard
Shifting from 'What happened?' to 'What's ideal?' requires working against powerful instincts.

First, we're biologically wired to scan for problems. Remember: threats always come first. When someone brings you a problem, your instinctive system wants to analyze it thoroughly.

Second, we've been culturally trained that good coaching means being a "fixer." Redirecting to solutions without analyzing the problem can feel superficial or dismissive.

Third, when clients arrive upset, our empathy drives us to meet them in that emotional space. Redirecting toward possibility when they're expressing pain can feel like we're minimizing their experience.

Finally, solution-focused questions require more cognitive effort. "What happened?" just tumbles out. "What do you want instead?" requires staying within your intentional system, even as your client might be pulling you into their defensive spiral.

A note on this: solution-focused doesn't mean context-free. Sometimes you need a sentence or two of background to understand what you're working with. The goal isn't to cut people off mid-sentence and pivot to "What's ideal?" The goal is to get just enough context to orient yourself, then redirect toward possibility before you both sink into the drama. A few minutes of context can be valuable. Ten (or more!) minutes of rehashing is not.

Coaching With a Problem Focus

The Scenario: Sarah is training for a half-marathon and wants to improve her speed. Her training plan includes speed work once a week, but she keeps skipping those workouts. She's frustrated because her race is in six weeks, and she's not seeing the improvement she wants.

Coach: "Last time we met, you were going to try and get two speed workouts in before we met again. What happened?"

Sarah: "I just... I can't seem to make myself do them. The easy runs are fine, but when it's speed day, I find excuses."

Coach: "What kind of excuses?"

Sarah: "Like, I'm too tired. Or the weather isn't great. Or I didn't sleep well. Sometimes I just look at the workout and think, 'I can't do that,' and go for an easy run instead."

Coach: "What makes you think you can't do the workouts?"

Sarah: "Well, last Tuesday I was supposed to do 800s, but I'd been up late the night before and I just knew I wouldn't hit the paces. And then Thursday I looked at the workout and it was supposed to be tempo intervals, and I haven't done those in months, so I figured I'd just fail anyway. And the week before that..."

Coach: "So what's getting in the way?"

Sarah: [Sighing] "I guess I just need more discipline."

Coach: "What makes you say you're not disciplined?"

Sarah: [Shoulders slumping] "Maybe I'm scared I'll fail. Or maybe I'm just lazy."

Coach: "Where do you think that fear comes from?"

Sarah: [Visibly deflated] "I don't know. Maybe I'm just not cut out for this."

What's happening here: The coach asked "What happened?" and got exactly what that question delivers: a spiral into drama, details, and storytelling about failure. Notice how Sarah's language shifts from "I can't seem to make myself do them" to "maybe I'm just not cut out for this." The problem-focused questions activated her defensive mode, triggered shame, and reinforced limiting beliefs. She's now more discouraged than when she started, and no closer to completing a speed workout.

Coaching With a Solutions Focus

The Scenario: The same situation with Sarah.

Coach: "I hear you're frustrated. You want to get faster, and you're not doing the workouts that would help you get there. What do you want from our conversation today?"

Sarah: "I need to figure out how to do these speed workouts. My race is in six weeks, and I'm running out of time."

Coach: "You want to show up for speed work so you can get faster for your race. That's a clear goal. Tell me about a speed workout you completed, even if it was just one. What was different that day?"

Sarah: [Pauses, thinking] "Actually, there was one about a month ago. It was 6x800 meters, and I crushed it. I felt really strong."

Coach: "You crushed it and felt strong, awesome! What made that day different?"

Sarah: [Energy lifting slightly] "I did it with my running group. We all met at the track, and there was this energy. Like we were all suffering together, but also cheering each other on, it was hard, but also kind of fun."

Coach: "So when you had community and accountability, the workout went from something you dreaded to something you enjoyed, even though it was still hard. What does that tell you?"

Sarah: "That I do better when I'm not alone? I've been trying to do all these workouts by myself, and I think I just talk myself out of them."

Coach: "What would it look like to create that community and accountability for more of your speed sessions?"

Sarah: [More engaged now, leaning forward] "My running group meets Tuesday evenings for track workouts. I could switch my speed day to Tuesday. Or I could ask one of my friends to meet me at the track on my scheduled day."

Coach: "Both of those sound doable. When you imagine showing up to your next speed workout with friends around you, all going through the same tough workout, how does that feel in your body?"

Sarah: "Way less intimidating. Like I could actually do it instead of just hoping I'll magically push myself."

Coach: "You already have the capability. You proved that when you crushed those 800s. You just need the conditions that help you access that capability. What's your next speed session, and how will you set yourself up for success?"

What's happening here: The coach acknowledged Sarah's frustration but immediately redirected toward her desired outcome. Instead of asking "What happened?" and diving into the problem, the coach asked about a time when it worked. By asking about a successful speed workout, the coach helped Sarah discover her own insight about what works for her. Notice how Sarah's language and energy shifted from "maybe I'm just not cut out for this" to "I could actually do it." The solution-focused questions kept her in discovery mode, where she could identify practical strategies rather than spiral into shame about her character flaws. The conversation took less time and delivered actionable insights.

What This Sounds Like in Practice

When you're practicing solution-focused coaching, you'll find yourself asking:

Instead of "What happened?":
- "What's ideal?"
- "What do you want instead?"
- "What do you want [the other person] to do?"
- "If this were solved, what would be different?"

To build on what's working:
- "What is already working?"
- "Was there ever a time when you were able to do this? What helped you succeed then?"
- "What would need to be true for this to succeed?"
- "What seems possible here?"

When reframing problem statements:
- "I keep failing at this." → "Tell me about a time you succeeded. What was different?"

- "I can't do X." → "What would doing X look like? When have you done something similar?"
- "I don't know why I'm avoiding this." → "What do you want to feel when this is done?"

Watch-Outs

You'll know you've slipped into problem-focus when you notice that you or your client are:

- Asking "What happened?"
- Stuck in a ten-minute (or longer!) vent session without pivoting toward a solution
- Watching your client's energy drain as they recount failures and excuses
- Feeling stuck or heavy yourself as you listen to gripe after gripe
- Thinking "We need to get to the root cause before we can move forward."
- Noticing your client becoming more discouraged, defensive, or self-blaming as the conversation continues

When you notice these patterns, pause and ask yourself: "What question would help them think about the solution right now?" Then pivot: "I want to shift gears for a moment. What's ideal here?"

Reflection Questions

➔ Bring to mind a challenge you're currently facing. Spend one minute thinking about it in problem-focused terms. Ask yourself what happened, and why, and what's perpetuating the issue? Notice how your body feels.

➔ Now spend one minute on the same challenge in solution-focused terms: What's ideal? What do you want instead?

When has something similar worked out for you? Notice how your body feels now. What changed?

→ Think about an upcoming coaching conversation. What's your automatic response when someone brings you a problem? Do you default to "What happened?" How might you replace that with "What's ideal?"

→ Practice catching yourself this week. Every time you're about to ask "What happened?" pause and ask a version of "What's ideal?" instead. Notice what happens in both your client's response and your own energy.

CHAPTER 8

Listen Generously

The Concept: The Power of "What Else?"

The shifts we've covered so far require you not only to ask better questions but also to become a better listener. However, what most people think of as active listening amounts to little more than parroting back what they heard. Making eye contact, nodding along, paraphrasing... "So what I'm hearing you say is..." These techniques demonstrate your attention, but if that's all you do in a conversation, you'll spend a lot of time going in circles.

Ultimately, coaching isn't just about talking about our thoughts, feelings, and actions. It's about changing them. And the way people change their lives is by taking different actions. As a coach, the way to propel a conversation from vision to insight to action is to listen generously, not just actively.

Here's why: active listening simply repeats content. It tells people what they already know. It stays at the surface. When you're coaching effectively, you're asking questions 90% of the time and making statements the other 10%. So what should you be doing in that critical 10% when you're not asking questions?

You're offering observations, reflections, and clarifications that add something to the conversation.

Think of your job as listening and looking for what the other person doesn't realize they are saying.

The goal of generous listening is to expand the opportunity for the client to learn something new about themselves that might unlock an insight and motivate action: a limiting belief to overcome, inner wisdom that can only emerge when given space, or an awareness of a feeling they just don't want to feel anymore. Generous listening expands and deepens the conversation so that the client learns something about themselves, the situation, or what life is trying to teach them.

Generous listening means you're not only hearing words. You're also observing patterns, noticing contradictions, tracking energy shifts, and listening for beliefs that underlie behavior. And then you reflect on what you notice in ways that help clients see themselves more clearly.

I see a lot of newer coaches get stuck in active listening and never contribute their own observations or interpretations because they're worried about getting it "wrong." And a lot of what I've shared about how easy it is to flip someone into a defensive state might give you pause. But we're talking about less than a tenth of the conversation.

And here's the most liberating part: you don't have to get it "right." Even when your reflection feels "wrong" to them at first, you've still given your client something to react to, which often helps them clarify their own thinking.

You say something like, "It sounds like you're frustrated with your colleague's lack of accountability, and you want to find a way to address it without causing conflict. Is that right?" And they say, "Well, no, I'm not averse to conflict, the problem is more that it's nearly impossible to get on his calendar..." You've still moved the conversation closer to what's really going on.

A person's initial answer to any question is rarely the one that sparks an insight or motivates action. That's because they've likely told themselves that very same thing thousands of times before and been unable to act on it. First responses are automatic, habitual, and reflect what we already know. The answers they've told themselves before. The explanations others have given them. The answer they think is the "right" one based on prior experience.

Sometimes we experience a first response as a "gut instinct," and sometimes those instincts are correct. I've tried hard in this book not to make the instinctive system seem "bad" and our intentional system "good" because sometimes our instincts do reflect our inner truth. But ultimately, we'll generate better ideas by engaging both systems of thinking.

This is why "What else?" is one of the most powerful questions a coach can ask. It signals: "Keep going. There's more here." Each time you request a version of "What else?" you move your client further from automatic reactivity and into more profound reflection.

The Three Facets of Generous Listening
Generous listening isn't one skill. It's three integrated capabilities working together:
1. **Observe beneath the surface:** Notice what they don't realize they're saying
2. **Reflect what you observe:** Name the patterns, contradictions, and energy shifts
3. **Invite clarification:** Use clarifying statements and questions to propel the conversation forward

Let's break down each facet. In the pages that follow, I'll return to the same examples to show how each facet builds on the last. You'll see how to notice something, then how to reflect it back, then how to use it to move the conversation forward.

Facet 1: Observe Beneath the Surface

Your job as a coach isn't only to listen to the words your client is saying. Your job is to notice and reflect back what they don't realize they're saying or even thinking.

Here's what to look and listen for:

Patterns of limiting beliefs. We all have ways of looking at ourselves, our work, other people, and the world that are helpful to where we want to go. And we also have unhelpful beliefs. Often, belief patterns reveal themselves in the form of repetition: words or phrases they repeat without realizing it.

I recently had a client describe himself as lazy three times in one conversation about building an exercise habit. When I brought up the frequent use of that label, he didn't even realize he was thinking that way about himself. That allowed him to reflect on what he really thought of himself: not that he was lazy about exercise, but rather that he was overly taxed in other areas of his life. He was managing quite a lot, which made him anything but lazy. This shifted the conversation toward exploring what he could take off his plate to make time for his health.

Contradictory beliefs. F. Scott Fitzgerald famously said, "The test of a first-rate intelligence is the ability to hold two opposing ideas in the mind at the same time and still retain the ability to function." It's one of the most frustrating and beautiful realities of being human. We are almost always thinking some version of "On one hand, I believe _____. But on the other hand, I believe the complete opposite to be true."

I once had a client who had trained for a marathon while managing a demanding executive role and raising two small children. Not ten minutes after telling me her backstory, she described one project at work as "too much for her to handle." On one hand, she viewed herself as extraordinarily capable, but on the other hand, completely incapable. Both versions were "true" to her at some level.

For that reason, I don't like to label thoughts as good or bad. They're all information, and they're all useful. The power lies in being able to look at contradictory beliefs objectively and accept that both exist. To make the changes we want, we must turn down the volume on unhelpful beliefs and turn up the ones that support the changes we're trying to make.

Shifts in energy. When a person's voice lifts, their posture relaxes, or their face lights up, you're witnessing a spark of genuine motivation or connection to something meaningful. Conversely, when they physically contract (shoulders creeping toward their ears, voice lowering, body language closing), you're seeing a signal that the conversation has touched on something emotionally charged: fear, shame, resistance, or discomfort. Both types of energy shifts tell you that you've hit on something significant and worth exploring further.

I worked with a client who was feeling stuck in her career. As she walked me through her path to her current role as a nonprofit director, her tone was flat. But the moment she mentioned a side project teaching design thinking workshops, her entire demeanor transformed. She sat forward, her eyes lit up, and she started talking with her hands. When I reflected on what I observed ("I notice your whole energy just shifted when you mentioned those workshops"), she paused and said, "I guess I hadn't realized how much that work actually matters to me." That observation opened a conversation about what she really wanted her career to be about.

A disconnect between words and body. One of the most revealing things to observe is when someone's words say one thing, but their body tells a different story. Saying "I'm excited about this opportunity" in a flat voice. Claiming "It's fine, I can handle it" while their jaw clenches. These disconnects often point to unacknowledged feelings or truths the client hasn't become aware of. They're telling you what they think they should feel while their body reveals what they actually feel.

I had a client who kept insisting she was "totally on board" with a restructuring that would give her more leadership responsibility. Her words were all positive, but every time she talked about it, she sat back in her chair and looked down at her lap. When I gently reflected, "Your body language seems to sort of check out even though you say you're on board. Are you on board?" She admitted she was terrified of failing in a more visible role. That shifted the conversation in a more productive and impactful direction, toward building her confidence and overcoming her fear of judgment.

Clues about their relationship with change or challenge. Coaching conversations exist because something needs to change. And change is hard. How someone talks about difficulty reveals essential information about what might get in their way or propel them forward. Listen for when their mind starts creating narratives about difficulty: Do they anticipate discomfort before it even arrives? What stories do they tell themselves when things get hard? And critically, what's the gap between what their mind is saying and what they're actually capable of doing?

I've been working with an experienced marathoner training to qualify for Boston. Like many distance runners, she frequently does progression runs: workouts that start at an easy pace and get progressively faster until the final miles are genuinely uncomfortable. Early on, I asked her to pay attention during these runs to where her mind goes when things start to get hard. She discovered something fascinating: her mind began catastrophizing during the first mile, while she was still running at a leisurely pace. "This is going to be terrible." "I'm not going to make it." The discomfort hadn't even set in yet, but her mind was already writing the story of her failure. When she pushed through to the harder miles, she found her body was far more capable than her mind had predicted.

She recognized the same pattern in her life beyond running: dreading difficult conversations before they happened, imagining worst-case scenarios before meetings even started. Once she could see how her mind related to challenge, she could separate the narrative from reality and choose a different response.

Lightbulb moments. When someone says, "I've never thought about it that way before..." or "It just dawned on me that..." or even just pauses with a visible shift in their expression, you're witnessing the moment a new insight has sparked. This is one of the most critical junctures in a coaching conversation because it signals that something has shifted internally.

Recognize this as a pivot point. The conversation needs to shift gears: either toward exploring concrete ways forward, or toward helping them anchor this new awareness, or deeper into what's motivating this insight and why it matters.

I worked with a client struggling with saying no to requests at work. Mid-conversation, she suddenly stopped and said, "Oh... I just realized I'm not actually worried about letting people down. I'm worried they'll think less of *me*." That pause, that "oh" moment, was the insight. Instead of quickly affirming it and moving forward, I asked, "What does that realization make possible for you?" She realized that if the real issue was her need for approval rather than genuinely disappointing others, she could work on managing her own reaction rather than trying to control others' perceptions by saying yes to everything. The lightbulb moment isn't the end. It's the beginning of a new conversation.

The Science Behind It

Remember what we learned about the two systems of thinking? When someone answers a question, their first response is almost always instinctive, drawing on what they already know, what they've thought before, and what they believe is the "right" answer. This is neurologically efficient but creatively limited. The instinctive system isn't designed to generate new insights. It's designed to recognize patterns and respond quickly. If their existing thought patterns had solved the problem, they wouldn't need coaching.

But here's what happens when you ask "What else?" or reflect something they didn't realize they were saying: you're inviting their intentional system to come online. That slower, more deliberate system is capable of integrating disparate information, considering multiple perspectives, and generating genuinely new connections.

This is also why generous listening requires you to operate from your own intentional system. When you're just parroting back what someone said, your instinctive system can handle that on autopilot. But noticing patterns, contradictions, and energy shifts? That requires you to stay cognitively engaged, resisting the urge to zone out or plan your next question while they're talking.

Research on metacognition confirms what most of us sense intuitively: we have significant blind spots about our own thinking. We can spot others' patterns and limiting beliefs far more easily than our own. When you reflect back what you observe ("I've noticed you've called yourself lazy three times" or "Your energy completely shifted when you mentioned that project"), you help clients see their own thinking from a distance. This psychological distance is what enables insight and choice rather than instinctive reaction.

And critically, generous listening helps keep you both in discovery mode. When someone feels truly seen and understood (not just heard, but understood at a deeper level), their nervous system registers safety. They remain in the state where growth is actually possible.

But here's what happens when you simply repeat back their words without adding observations: the conversation circles. They keep telling you what they already know. They stay in their instinctive patterns. Most importantly, they don't learn anything new about themselves.

Why This Is Hard

Generous listening requires working against several powerful instincts:

The information load of attending to multiple sources at once. You're listening to the surface level of what the person is saying while simultaneously watching for patterns and disconnects. That's a lot of information to process, especially if what they're saying doesn't match what you're seeing. It's much easier to take their response at face value.

Tolerating contradictions. Our brains prefer consistency and want to resolve tension by deciding which belief is "true." But insight comes from holding both as accurate simultaneously and helping the client choose which one serves their future.

Having the courage to share what you observe. It feels vulnerable to name what you're noticing, especially when it might be "wrong." We've been conditioned to believe we should only speak when we're certain. But your observations move the conversation forward, even when they miss the mark. Staying silent because you're not sure is almost always the less useful choice.

Asking "What else?" when you think you already understand. Staying curious enough to keep asking requires conscious effort and patience. Both you and the client's instinctive system want to move forward with the first answer. You will have to manage your own impatience while also tolerating some impatience on the client's part. As clients see the benefits of coaching over time and get that hit of satisfaction from an "aha" moment, they become more patient and naturally accept this style of conversation.

Facet 2: Reflect What You Observe

The real power of generous listening is in how you reflect what you've noticed in a way that gives them something additional to consider. The goal isn't to interpret or diagnose, but to hold up a mirror so they can see themselves more clearly. When done well, these reflections offer your client opportunities to learn more about themselves and to unlock a meaningful way forward.

Here's how you might reflect on each type of observation:

When you notice patterns of limiting beliefs: "I've noticed that you've used the term 'lazy' three times in this conversation. I'm curious about that view of yourself. What comes up when I point that out?" You're naming the pattern, identifying it as a belief, and inviting them to look at it with you.

When you notice contradictory beliefs: "I'm hearing that on one hand you see yourself as someone who trained for a marathon while managing an executive role and raising two kids. Extraordinarily capable. But on the other hand, you're describing one difficult project as "too much to handle." They both sound true to you, but they strike me as opposite thoughts. What do you make of that?" You're holding up both beliefs without judgment and inviting them to examine which way of looking at the situation or themselves will make them more resourceful.

When you notice shifts in energy: "I notice your whole energy just shifted when you mentioned those workshops. Your voice picked up, and you leaned forward. That says to me that there's something about that work that lights you up. Am I reading that right?" You're naming the physical change, connecting it to meaning, and checking your understanding.

When you notice a disconnect between words and body: "You're telling me you're ready for this additional responsibility, but your body language seems guarded. Your arms are crossed, your voice has an edge. What are you feeling in your body as you talk about it?" You're pointing out the contradiction and inviting them to explore what their instincts are trying to tell them.

When you notice clues about their relationship with challenge: "I'm noticing that when you talk about this difficult conversation you need to have, your mind is already anticipating the worst before it even happens. I'm wondering if that's a pattern for you. Is there anywhere else in your life where this shows up?" You're naming the anticipatory anxiety, suggesting it might be broader, and inviting them to see where else it appears.

When you notice a lightbulb moment: Explicitly pause and mark the new idea as significant. "I want to pause here because this seems like a significant shift. You've been talking about how hard it is to say no, and how you worry about letting people down. But what you just said: "I'm not actually worried about letting people down. I'm worried they'll think less of me"...that feels like a big 'aha' to me. What do you make of that?" You've named the insight back to them and marked it as significant, allowing you to pivot toward new possibilities.

Facet 3: Invite Clarification

When you're practicing generous listening, you'll find yourself saying things like:

Reflecting patterns: "This is the third time you've mentioned..." "Every time you talk about X, you..." "I notice that when you describe Y, your energy shifts...What do you make of that?"

Reflecting contradictions: "Earlier you said X, but now you're saying Y. Those two things seem to contradict each other. What do you think?"

Clarifying with interpretation: "Let me see if I understand what's really happening here..." "So if I'm hearing you correctly, this isn't about X. It's actually about Y. Am I close?" "What I'm hearing is XYZ... Does that land?"

Naming energy and body signals: "I noticed your shoulders just dropped when..." "Your whole energy lifted when you said...", "You're saying you're excited, but your body language seems less excited...what else is going on?"

Using "What else?" to go deeper: "What else is true?" "What else are you noticing?"

Clarifying statements: "Tell me more about that." "Help me understand what you mean by..." "It would help me if you'd give me an example."

The pattern is always the same: observation ("I notice..."), interpretation ("It sounds like..." or "I'm wondering if..."), and invitation ("Does that sound right?" "Am I close?" "What do you make of that?"). This three-part structure ensures you're not just telling them what you think. You're offering your perspective as something for them to consider and respond to.

The Power of Being "Wrong"

When I teach people how to coach, this is often the part where the energy gets heavy. When I suggest that people add generous observations to their clarifying statements, they usually feel trepidation around getting it wrong.

But here is the good news: even when your clarification is "wrong," it's useful.

When you offer a reflection, even if it doesn't completely resonate with the client, you're still giving them something to respond to. Their response will always sharpen your focus, both of you, on what's really going on beneath the surface.

Consider this example:

Coach: "So it sounds like you're avoiding delegating this report because you're worried your team won't execute it as well as you would, and that might reflect negatively on you. Is that right?"

Client: "Actually... no. I think they'd probably do it better than me at this point, if I'm being honest. I think it's more that this is the one thing I get to actually do, as opposed to just overseeing. It's actually fun to sit down and do the report myself. I miss doing the real work."

See what happened? The coach makes a reasonable assumption (quality concerns are a common delegation barrier), but being slightly off forces the client to articulate what's actually true. And in that correction, the client discovers something they hadn't quite named before: this isn't about trust or capability. It's about identity and purpose.

The misfire becomes productive because it creates contrast. The client has to say "no, not that," which naturally leads them to "so what IS it then?" Suddenly, they're at a much deeper level than where they started.

This happens all the time in good coaching. You don't need to be perfectly accurate with every reflection. Often, missing the mark is more useful than being silent, because it gives the client something to respond to and refine.

This is why clarifying is always valuable. You don't need to be perfectly accurate. You need to be observant enough to notice something beneath the surface; brave enough to name what you're seeing; and humble enough to hold your interpretation lightly.

The goal isn't perfection. It's generosity. You're adding your observations and interpretations to the conversation, trusting that even when you miss the mark, you're still moving the dialogue forward.

Coaching With "Active" but not Generous Listening

The Scenario: Rachel has been wanting to launch her own consulting business for a couple of years. She works full-time and is looking at this side business as an extra stream of income until she builds it to a point where she can leave her job.

Coach: "What do you think would help you get started?"

Rachel: "I just don't have enough time. Between my full-time job and my kids, there aren't enough hours in the day. I need to build my website, create my service packages, and develop my marketing strategy. It's overwhelming."

Coach: "That does sound like a lot. So what I'm hearing you say is that you need more time. What would help you find more time?"

Rachel: "I don't know. Maybe I need to wake up earlier? But I'm already exhausted. I'm just not disciplined enough to make this happen."

Coach: "Okay, so you're thinking you could wake up earlier. What would that look like?"

Rachel: "I guess I could try setting my alarm for 5 AM? But honestly, now that the kids are older, I can't get myself to bed until almost 11, and I'm exhausted already."

Coach: "I hear you. Let's think through your schedule. Walk me through a typical day. Where could you potentially carve out time?"

Rachel: "Well, I wake up at 6:30, get the kids ready, commute, work until 5:30, pick up the kids, make dinner, help with homework, and by 8:30 I'm wiped out. Sometimes I'll try to work on the business after the kids go to bed, but I just stare at the screen. I'm terrible at this."

Coach: "What about weekends? Is there time there?"

Rachel: "Saturdays are soccer and errands. Sundays I try to meal prep and get ready for the week. I keep telling myself I'll find time, but I never do. Maybe I'm just not meant to be an entrepreneur."

What's happening here: The coach is practicing active listening: parroting back Rachel's words ("so what I'm hearing you say is..."), asking follow-up questions about the surface issue. But they're missing everything beneath the surface. They didn't notice that Rachel called herself "not disciplined enough," "terrible at this," and questioned whether she's "meant to be an entrepreneur." Three versions of "I'm not capable." They missed the energy draining from Rachel as the conversation progressed. They let her spiral into recounting everything wrong, reinforcing her sense of impossibility. And when they finally contributed something, it was advice about what worked for them, not an observation about what's really happening for Rachel. The conversation circles without forward movement. Active listening kept them at the surface while the real motivation, and fears, remained invisible.

Coaching With Generous Listening

The Scenario: The same situation with Rachel.

Coach: "You want to launch your consulting business. Tell me what that would give you."

Rachel: "Freedom. Flexibility. I actually get to choose which clients I work with. No more corporate politics."

Coach: [Noticing energy shift] "When you just said 'freedom' and 'flexibility,' your whole energy lifted. Did you notice that?"

Rachel: [Pausing] "I did, actually. It's really important to me, so I'm frustrated that I've been talking about it for two years and haven't actually done it."

Coach: "When you think about the actual work of launching (building the website, creating your offering), what happens in your body?"

Rachel: [Shoulders dropping, voice flattening] "It feels heavy. Like I'm pushing a boulder uphill."

Coach: "So the vision feels expansive and energizing, but the path feels heavy. Tell me more about that heaviness."

Rachel: "I just don't have enough time. Between my full-time job and the kids, I'm already exhausted."

Coach: "What else besides managing the exhaustion could make this feel easier?"

Rachel: "I'm not disciplined enough. I should be able to make time, but I just... don't."

Coach: "What else?"

Rachel: [Longer pause] "I think... I think I'm scared. At my corporate job, I know what I'm doing. I'm good at it. But starting my own thing? What if I'm not actually good enough to make it work?"

Coach: "There it is. What you've been calling a time problem or a discipline problem is actually fear. And that makes complete sense. You're considering leaving the safety of something you've mastered for the uncertainty of something new. Of course that's scary."

Rachel: [Tearing up slightly] "Yeah. It really is."

Coach: "I want to point something out. A contradiction I'm noticing. You just described yourself as 'not disciplined enough.' But you've sustained a demanding corporate role for twelve years while raising two kids. You're not only still standing, but you're still performing incredibly well. That sounds like extraordinary discipline to me. What do you make of that?"

Rachel: [Quiet] "I never thought of it that way. I guess I am disciplined when it comes to things that are already... established."

Coach: "So if I'm hearing you correctly, you've proven you have discipline when it comes to sustaining existing commitments. The challenge isn't discipline itself. It's something about starting something brand new that feels different. Am I close?"

Rachel: [Leaning forward now] "Yes. When you put it like that... I know I have the expertise. I've built campaigns that worked for Fortune 500 companies. I've solved impossible problems. But I still hear this voice saying 'what if you can't do it this time?'"

Coach: "One part of you knows you have valuable expertise that's solved complex problems for major companies. Another part is asking, 'What if I'm not good enough?' Both feel true, don't they?"

Rachel: "They do. That's the frustrating part."

Coach: "Here's what I know about contradictory beliefs: we all have them, all the time, about nearly everything. Both sides of the same story seem completely true to us, even if they are complete opposites. The question isn't which one is right or wrong because they're both real, and both give us good information. The question is: which one serves the future you're trying to create? When you think about yourself as someone with valuable expertise launching a business, what becomes possible?"

Rachel: "I could actually do this. Not perfectly, but I could start. I could take one step."

Coach: "What's one small step that would help turn the volume up on that more helpful belief? The one that says you have what it takes?"

What's happening here: The coach practiced generous listening from the start, observing Rachel's energy shift when talking about freedom versus the heavy feeling around launching. They asked "What else?" multiple times to move Rachel past her surface explanations (time, discipline) to the real issue (fear of not being good enough). They identified two contradictions: between Rachel's claim that she lacks discipline and her proven track record, and between her fear of inadequacy and her demonstrated expertise. They offered clarifying statements that added interpretation: "What you've been calling a time problem is actually fear." Even when the clarifications might not have been perfectly accurate, they gave Rachel something to react to, deepening the conversation.

Watch-Outs

You'll know you've stayed at the surface or missed opportunities for generous listening when you notice:

- *Accepting the first answer without exploring:* If you're moving forward with initial responses, you're likely missing deeper insights. When you hear a quick answer, that's your cue to ask "What else?"

- *Just paraphrasing content:* If you're only reflecting words ("So what I'm hearing is...") without adding observation or interpretation, you're practicing active listening but not generous listening.

- *Circling without movement:* If you're feeling lost in a rambling story, or returning to the same issue session after session without progress, step back and ask yourself: what am I noticing that I haven't named yet?

- *Missing energy shifts:* If a session passes without noticing moments when energy shifts (expansion or contraction), bring your attention back to what you're seeing and sensing, not just hearing.

- *Being afraid to be wrong:* If you're only sharing observations when you're certain, you're missing opportunities. Offer your interpretation tentatively and trust that even if you're off, you've given them something to react to.

When you catch yourself in any of these patterns, pause and ask yourself: "What am I noticing but not naming? What question would help them go deeper? What interpretation might I offer, even tentatively?"

Reflection Questions

→ Practice noticing your own patterns. For the next few days, pay attention to the language you use about yourself when you're challenged or uncomfortable. What words do you repeat? What do these phrases tell you about the beliefs you're carrying?

→ Spot your own contradictions. Think of an area where you feel stuck. Write down beliefs you have about yourself and the situation, both helpful and unhelpful. Which beliefs would you want to strengthen?

→ Notice energy shifts. In your following conversation, pay attention to when the other person's energy shifts. When do they light up? When do they contract?

→ Watch for body-word mismatches. This week, observe when someone's words say one thing, but their body says another. Practice gently naming what you notice.

→ Practice "What else?" The next time someone gives you a quick answer to a meaningful question, resist the urge to respond. Instead, simply ask "What else?" See what emerges when you give them permission to go deeper.

→ Experiment with clarification. In your next coaching conversation, practice offering your interpretation even when you're not 100% certain. Try phrases like "I'm wondering if..." or "It sounds like... Am I close?" Notice what happens when you give them something to respond to.

CHAPTER 9

When Coaching Gets Hard

This Isn't Therapy.

One of the most common concerns I hear from clients early in a coaching relationship is that this method feels a lot like therapy, and they don't want therapy. I understand why. Because I'm asking questions rather than giving advice, there's a similar feeling of being on the hot seat, of someone probing into your thoughts and emotions. It can feel vulnerable.

Where therapy and coaching overlap is that both rely on questions and aim to uncover belief systems to shift how someone thinks, works, and lives. But there's a crucial difference. Therapy is often focused on the root cause. How did you come to think and behave this way? What happened in your past that created this pattern? It frequently looks backward, especially at painful or formative experiences.

Coaching is focused solely on the future. The solution. The ideal. While past experiences may come up, your role is to guide clients toward *who they want to become*. How do they *want to* feel, think, and act?

There's another reason clients sometimes resist this approach. They think they want to be told what to do. "You know best," they'll say. "Just tell me what to do." But as we've covered, advice doesn't create lasting change. They need to discover it for themselves. Your job is to hold that boundary, even when they push against it.

Still, there are times when coaching isn't the right intervention.

For professional coaching relationships, I strongly recommend a coaching agreement that both you and the client sign. Mine includes this language: "*As your coach, I cannot guarantee results. You will create powerful results by having the courage and determination to take action in your life. I am trained as a coach, not as a psychotherapist or physician, and I am not trained in diagnosing psychological or medical conditions. If any issues come up for you that should be handled by a licensed therapist or physician, I will insist that you attend to your health by contacting the appropriate professional.*"

A handful of times in my career, I've been in conversation with someone who is consistently overtaken by their emotions in a way that makes forward-thinking conversation impossible. Sometimes they describe events that any reasonable person would recognize as traumatic, or they show visible signs of a traumatic response: flash-backs, dissociation during our conversation, or being so on edge they can't stay present.

Here are some common red flags that signal a client may need more support than coaching can provide:

- Mentions of suicidal thoughts, self-harm, or a desire to "disappear" or "not be here anymore"
- Signs of active crisis: inability to function at work or home, not sleeping or eating, acute distress that doesn't stabilize
- Substance use that's interfering with their ability to show up, follow through, or think clearly

- Disordered eating patterns or obsessive thoughts about food, weight, or body image
- Paranoid thinking or beliefs that seem disconnected from reality
- Mentions of current or recent abuse, either as the person experiencing it or perpetrating it
- Use of abusive or threatening language or body posture toward you
- Panic attacks that are frequent or escalating
- Depression so heavy they can't engage with future-focused questions at all

When I notice these signs, I gently ask how they're taking care of themselves. Whether they're currently under the care of a physician. Whether they're on any medications. And in a few cases, I've made the decision to stop working with someone and suggested they speak with a psychiatrist or therapist instead.

This isn't a failure of coaching. It's a recognition that coaching has boundaries, and honoring those boundaries is part of serving your client well.

One note on abusive or threatening behavior: if a client uses threatening language or adopts a physically intimidating posture toward you, do not try to de-escalate or gently probe. End the session immediately and remove yourself from the situation. Your safety comes first. This is non-negotiable. You can address what happened later (or not at all), but at the moment, your only job is to get yourself somewhere safe.

When They Don't Want to Be There
As a professional coach, you will occasionally be commissioned to work with someone who doesn't want coaching. This happens even

more frequently when you're a manager. Either way, the approach is similar.

When a leader brings you someone to coach, it's usually because they value a lot about the person. They want to keep them because of their institutional knowledge, because of the cost to replace them, because they want them to develop new capabilities for a bigger role, or simply because they believe the person's strengths outweigh their weaknesses.

Often the conversation sounds something like 'This person is AMAZING, but…"

But the person being coached didn't ask for this. When coaching is suggested or imposed, it often triggers resistance.

Here's how I handle it.

First, contract with the person commissioning the coaching work that you will need to meet with the person before committing to the engagement. You want time to assess whether a productive coaching relationship is possible. Both you and the potential client need to be able to evaluate fit.

Second, establish trust. You must be able to promise confidentiality: everything you discuss stays between the two of you. You will never speak for them or report back to anyone about your conversations. This is a deal you must make with whoever is commissioning the coaching, and if they don't agree, walk away. Even if it means turning down a paying client.

Third, try to shift them into discovery mode from the start. One way to do this is by framing the engagement as a vote of confidence. Their company is investing in them. Someone believes in their potential enough to bring in outside support. That reframe can soften initial resistance.

If you're a manager rather than an external coach, steps one and two obviously don't apply in the same way. You can't promise the same level of confidentiality. But you can still assess whether someone is ready for coaching and decide how much time to invest. That's where coachability comes in.

As a coach or manager, you need a framework for assessing whether someone is ready for coaching. If you're a professional coach, this helps you decide whether to take them on. If you're a manager, it enables you to gauge how much of your time to invest. You want to set yourself up for success, and taking on an uncoachable client won't do that.

Fortunately, most people are coachable. A good coach can help someone make nearly any change they want in life. By asking the right questions, listening generously, and knowing when and how to propel the conversation toward action, it doesn't matter whether you're an expert in running, finance, weight loss, or whatever their goal is. If you're a skilled coach, and they're a ready and willing client, the relationship will be productive.

It only takes two things to make someone coachable.

One: They have to want something to be different. There has to be some gap between where they are and where they want to be that they actually care about closing.

Two: They have to believe they have the power to effect change in their own life. We've all met people who see themselves as victims of circumstance. In a coaching context, that posture makes progress impossible. You're not coaching their boss, coworker, spouse, or family of origin. You're only working with them. And they have to feel agency over their own life and circumstances.

If both of those elements are present, even someone who arrived reluctantly can become a deeply engaged client. If either is missing, you'll be pushing a boulder uphill.

When Emotions Run High

Sometimes a client shows up in distress. Tears, anger, frustration, or just a flood of words about something that happened since you last spoke. This is normal. Life doesn't pause for coaching sessions.

When someone is highly emotionally charged, their emotional brain has hijacked their intentional system. At that moment, coaching is not possible. You cannot ask future-focused, creative questions of someone whose nervous system is in full defensive mode.

But that doesn't necessarily mean the session is lost. Your job is to give them space without rescuing them, and then help them return to a state where coaching can proceed.

Here's what a momentary emotional flare-up usually looks like: they move in and out of the heightened emotional state. One second, there are tears or sharp edges to their words. In the next breath, they say something like "but anyway" or "sorry, that's not what we're here to talk about." They're toggling between the emotional flood and their social awareness that they're in a coaching session.

When I see this, I give them explicit permission to let it out. I'll say something like, "It's okay. I think it's important that you clear out anything in your brain that's standing in the way of you being fully present here. Go ahead and tell me what's going on."

Then I let them go. I don't interrupt. I don't try to fix it. I don't offer reassurance or perspective. I just listen until they start to slow down on their own. Usually, they'll make a transitional statement: "Anyway." "Thank you for listening." "I just needed to vent."

You'll know they're coming back to center when you see it in their body. Their words slow down. Their breathing deepens. The edge of anger or the weepiness subsides. When I notice that shift, I'll name what I heard and give them a choice about where to go next.

"I just heard you mention X, Y, and Z that seem to be heavily on your mind. Is that something you'd like to set aside for the sake of this conversation, and we can start where we left off last time? Or is this something you'd like some coaching on today?"

Sometimes what they vent about becomes the session. If I see an obvious connection to what we've been working on, I'll name it: "Last time you said you wanted to be bolder with setting expectations with your employees. This situation with Kevin seems like a good place to pick up on that. What do you think?"

Sometimes I'll set a gentle time limit upfront: "Why don't we spend five minutes, no more than ten, with you just getting it all out of your system. Then we'll proceed with the rest of the session."

But occasionally, someone isn't able to come back to center. The intensity doesn't subside. They keep looping on the same point, or the emotion keeps escalating rather than settling. In those cases, I gently require that we postpone the conversation to another day. This isn't a failure. It's a recognition that the purpose of coaching is to help people think creatively so they can take action on what's important in their lives, and that at that moment, the conditions aren't right. The kindest thing you can do is give them time and space rather than push forward into a conversation that can't be productive.

PART III

THE
MODEL

You now understand the four practices: regarding clients as resourceful and whole, asking instead of telling, focusing on solutions instead of problems, and listening generously. You know the science behind why they matter. And you've seen examples of what each one looks like in action.

In this final section, we're going to put all the science and skills together into a model for leading coaching conversations. The VITAL coaching model is a roadmap that moves through five stages: envisioning the ideal, tapping into inner motivation, exploring possible ways forward, designing actionable next steps, and making it stick.

VITAL gives you a clear structure for coaching conversations while remaining flexible enough to respond to new insights and ideas that emerge along the way. Each letter represents a distinct phase that builds on the last:

V - Vision: Start with developing a shared understanding of what is ideal for them. Where do they want to go? Who do they want to be? How do they want to grow or change? You want to land on the one or two changes that, if they could make meaningful progress on them, would make the most significant difference in their life.

I - Insight: What is underneath that vision? What would it mean for them if they could achieve it? Who would they become? What significance does that have in their life? Listen for that "aha" moment that indicates a spark of inner motivation.

T - Tactics: Explore all the possible tactics for moving their vision forward. This is an ideation phase. The first idea (or two or three) they have might come from old belief systems or narratives about how they "should" be. In this phase you'll invite them to consider not only their instinctual reactions but also other perspectives.

A - Action: From there, you'll work together to design actions that balance being a stretch out of their comfort zone while also being likely to happen. What's the next right thing to try? Both you and the client should approach action planning with curiosity: what new habit or way of being would they like to try on? What are they hoping to learn from that?

L - Learning: Based on what changes they try out, you'll work together to identify key wins, explore what they learned about themselves, and determine what's next. The VITAL coaching model is circular. Every new thing the client tries is an opportunity to teach them something and a chance to refine what is ideal. Every conversation about Learning becomes an opportunity to feed the next Vision.

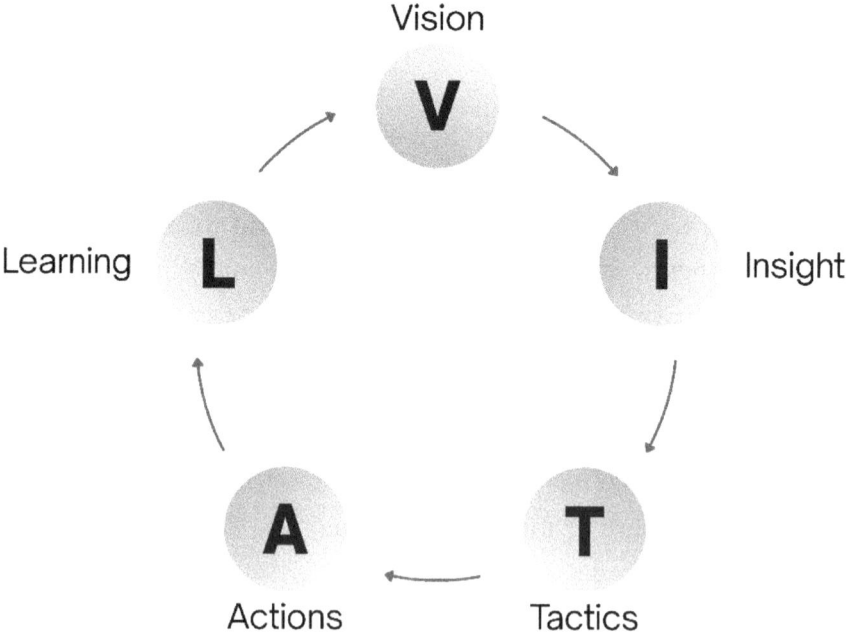

Vision

V

Learning **L**   **I** Insight

A   **T**

Actions   Tactics

Here's what makes this model powerful: it's built on everything you've learned about how to help people do their best thinking.

When you start with Vision, you're keeping your client in discovery mode. Imagining one's future ideal self is more exciting than cataloging everything you want to fix. The Insight phase is where you go deeper, uncovering what lies beneath that vision and why it truly matters. When you explore Tactics together, you're helping them generate ideas about what's possible and engaging their creativity to look at solutions from different perspectives. Action planning allows them to reinforce helpful belief systems and try on new ones. Learning anchors those wins, strengthening the beliefs that will keep them moving forward.

You can use the VITAL coaching model as a roadmap for your coaching conversations. In your first session, you'll likely move through all five phases and aim to end with one or two action items. But in your next conversation, you might start with Learning. What did they try? What did they not try? And what did they learn from that? Take that Learning and go back to Vision because Learning shapes new Vision. Each conversation builds on the last, creating momentum that compounds over time.

And here's the crucial part: throughout this book, we've been talking about listening for lightbulb moments.

While only one phase is called Insight, you're actually listening for those "aha" moments through the entire conversation. They're the pivot points that signify when you should move to the next phase.

In the Insight phase specifically, you're listening for that spark of inner motivation that fuels everything that comes after. Without it, Action planning becomes just another list of shoulds that your client struggles to follow through on. With it, Action feels almost inevitable because it's connected to something they discovered for themselves.

One more thing before we dive in. What happens when the person doesn't take the action they set out to take? I always say, "Awesome!" There can be more to learn from the actions people don't take than the ones they do. When people come back week after week saying they want to do something but they're not doing it, that's a huge opportunity to learn something: maybe you landed on the wrong action item, maybe it was too much of a stretch, maybe it's butting up against a limiting belief that needs to be addressed first.

In the pages ahead, I'll walk you through each phase of the VITAL coaching model. For each one, you'll get the purpose, the questions to ask, what to look and listen for, and how to pivot to the next phase. Think of this as your field guide. Something you can reference before sessions, dog-ear for later, or even pull up on your phone when you're in the middle of a conversation and need a fresh option.

A word about those questions: each phase includes a list of them, but these aren't scripts to follow or boxes to check. Think of them as a menu of possibilities to choose from based on where the conversation goes. Using these questions flexibly helps you stay present and responsive. At any given moment, you're not thinking "What's the next question on the list?" You're thinking, "What question will help move the conversation forward?"

The phases themselves are equally flexible. You might spend an entire first session in Vision, helping someone get clear on what they actually want. Or you might move through all five phases in a fifteen-minute conversation with someone on your team between meetings. A coaching engagement that spans months will look very different from a single conversation in the hallway or on the sidelines, but the underlying structure is the same.

Over time, the goal is to internalize the intent behind each phase so profoundly that the right question comes up naturally when you need it. You won't be mentally consulting a list. You'll simply notice when someone is stuck in a limiting belief, or when they're ready to move from ideas to action, and the question will come.

CHAPTER 10

Setting Up the Coaching Relationship

Before you dive into the VITAL coaching model with a new client, there are a few things worth covering in your first conversation together.

First, clarify what they want from coaching. Not the specific goal yet, but what brought them to you. What's happening in their life or work that made them seek support? What are they hoping will be different six months from now?

Second, establish how you'll know it's working by asking: "If coaching is wildly successful, what will be different? How will you know?" This plants a seed for the Vision conversation while also creating shared accountability. You're not promising outcomes, but you're making sure you both understand what success looks like.

Third, cover the practical logistics: how often you'll meet, session length, contact between sessions, and your cancellation policy. For professional coaches, this is also when you sign your coaching agreement. A sample agreement is available at

www.jenniferfarrer.com.

Finally, name how you work. I usually say something like: "My approach is to ask you a lot of questions rather than give you advice. I believe you already have the answers you're looking for. My job is to help you find them." This sets expectations and prevents the "just tell me what to do" dynamic from taking hold.

All of this can happen in fifteen minutes. Then you're ready to begin.

CHAPTER 11

Vision

Purpose

The Vision phase is where you develop a shared understanding of what's ideal for your client. You're helping them articulate where they want to go, who they want to be, and how they want to grow or change. The goal is to land on one or two things that, if they could make meaningful progress on them, would make the biggest difference in their life.

But clarity alone isn't enough. You want to see the inspiration on their face and hear it in their voice. You'll know when you've struck something that lights them up. With an inspiring Vision as the North Star, they'll be compelled by inner motivation rather than feeling like the work is something they have to constantly push themselves to do.

Questions

Opening questions:

- "What would you like to focus on in our time together?"
- "If we sit together six months from now, looking back, and coaching has been a smashing success, what would that look like?"

- "What's one change that, if you were able to make significant progress on it, would make everything else in this part of your life easier or better?"
- "If you could wave a magic wand and change one thing about this situation, what would it be?"
- "What does your ideal work life/relationship/leadership style look like?"

Questions to uncover inner motivation
- "What is important to you about this?"
- "What draws you to these changes right now?"
- "What would it mean to you to become someone who had achieved this?"
- "How would that change the way you see yourself?"
- "How do you want to feel at the end of the day / when you wake up in the morning / on the other side of accomplishing this goal?"
- "On a scale of 1-10, how motivated do you feel right now to develop this vision? What makes it so motivating?"

Questions to help clarify their goal
- "What does that look like specifically?" *Use when they give abstract answers like "I want to be more confident" or "I want a better work-life balance."*
- "How would life look, sound, and feel if that became a reality?"
- "How would you know you've achieved that? What would be different?"
- "What would success look like for you?"
- "If you could have exactly what you wanted in this area of your life, what would that be?"

When they're stuck or giving surface-level answers

- "I'm hearing you say [repeat what they said]. Tell me more about that."
- "You mentioned [specific word or phrase they used]. What does that mean to you?"
- "That sounds like something you think you *should* want. What do you actually want?" *Use this when you hear "should" language or sense they're giving you the "right" answer.*
- "Let's try this differently. If no one was watching and you couldn't fail, what would you want?"
- "What would the most courageous version of yourself say right now?"

What to Look and Listen For

Energy shifts

- Watch for when their energy lifts: posture opens, voice rises, they lean forward or speak faster. These are signs you're getting closer to what actually matters to them.
- Notice when their energy drops: voice flattens, shoulders tense, they pull back or look away. This often signals you've touched on something uncomfortable but worth exploring.
- Pay attention to when their voice gets quieter or more tentative. This might mean they're sharing something vulnerable, or it might mean they're giving you what they think you want to hear.

Body language mismatches

- When they say "yes, that's it," but their body language is closed or uncertain, you haven't yet landed on the real vision. Try: "I'm noticing some hesitation. Let's get curious about that."

- If they're nodding enthusiastically but not making eye contact, they might be trying to convince themselves. Ask: "I hear what you're saying, but there's part of me that thinks maybe we haven't landed on exactly what you want yet. What do you think?"

Language patterns that signal readiness to move forward
- They use "I want" or "I will" language instead of "I should" or "I need to"
- They speak in the present or future tense about the vision, not the past tense about problems
- They describe their vision with specific, concrete details rather than vague generalities
- They can articulate their vision clearly in one or two sentences

Signs You Need to Stay Longer
- They keep circling back to what's wrong or what they want to avoid rather than what they're moving toward
- They use a lot of "I don't know" responses.
- Their vision is about fixing themselves rather than becoming who they want to be
- They can only describe what they don't want, not what they do want
- You hear a lot of "I should" statements or language that sounds like it's coming from someone else's expectations

When and How to Pivot
Move from Vision to Insight when:
- They can clearly and specifically articulate where they want to go
- You notice a shift in their energy when they describe their vision, indicating inner motivation

- They've stopped adding new elements when you ask, "What else?"
- They can describe their vision in concrete, vivid terms (not just abstract concepts)
- You hear them say things like "That would be amazing" or "It would make everything in my life easier or better" with genuine energy behind it.
- Their body language is open and engaged when talking about the vision

Use clarifying statements and questions like these to pivot to the Insight phase:

- "So it sounds like what you really want is [reflect their vision]. Is that right?"
- "I'm hearing that [summarize their vision]. Does that capture it?"
- "That's a powerful vision. What would it mean for you if you could actually make that happen?" (This is your bridge question into Insight)

CHAPTER 12

Insight

Purpose

The Insight phase is where you help your client think about their own thinking. Your goal is to develop a shared understanding of how they're currently seeing the situation they've brought into coaching: the lens through which they're viewing the challenge, the assumptions they're making, and the stories they're telling themselves.

As you explore together, you'll likely uncover limiting beliefs that are keeping them stuck. From there, you can begin opening up alternative perspectives: ways of seeing that feel more true, more useful, and more energizing. The aim is to land on one or two mental shifts that would make the change they're hoping for feel not just possible but natural.

This phase can be emotional, meaningful, and magical. When someone sees something they couldn't see before, when a belief they've carried for years suddenly loosens its grip, it can be the kind of lightbulb moment that stays with them for life. Everything downstream gets easier: the action, the follow-through, the lasting change. And beyond this single coaching engagement, they walk away with a mind that's a little more free.

Questions

Opening questions to surface their current thinking

- How have you been thinking about this [change/challenge/situation]?
- How clear are you on what it would take to…?
- What do you believe is true about this situation?
- What assumptions are you making?
- What's the story you're telling yourself about this?
- When you imagine yourself making this change, how does it feel?

Questions to gently loosen limiting beliefs

- What feelings come up for you when you think of it that way?
- Where do you feel that belief in your body?
- Usually, when we carry around a belief for a while, it's because it does serve us in some way. How is that belief serving you?
- What does that belief cost you?
- What would it feel like to set that belief down, even temporarily?
- What evidence do you have for that? What evidence do you have against it?*
- What's *really* true about this situation?

* Why I ask for evidence even for unhelpful beliefs: this may seem counterintuitive. Throughout this book, I've argued against activating your client's defenses, and asking someone to defend a belief they hold could do precisely that. So why do I ask?

Because when someone names a limiting belief, the evidence they cite is almost always surprisingly thin: one critical comment, one failed attempt, one person who made them feel small. Asking the question doesn't strengthen the belief. It exposes how little it's built on. And when you follow up with "what evidence do you have against it?", they usually discover a lifetime of contradictory experiences they've been discounting. The belief starts to feel less like an unchangeable truth and more like one interpretation, one they formed from limited data and have been carrying ever since.

Questions to open alternative perspectives
- Is there any part of you that feels differently?
- How else could you look at this?
- What would [someone they admire] say about this?
- What would you tell a good friend or your child if they were in this same situation?
- What would you have to believe about yourself to make this change feel easy?
- What if the opposite were true?
- What might you be missing?
- If this turned out to be easier than you thought, what would that mean about how you've been seeing it?

Questions to help them articulate their insight
- What are you realizing as we talk?
- What's shifting for you?
- What do you see now that you didn't see before?
- If you carried that new belief forward, what would change?
- It looks like something may have just dawned on you. What is that?

What to Look and Listen For

Limiting beliefs surfacing

- Watch for absolute language: "I always," "I never," "I can't," "That's just how I am." These phrases often signal a fixed belief that they've taken on as an identity.

- Listen for old stories. When they reference past failures or long-held narratives about themselves ("I've never been good at..."), you're getting close to something worth exploring.

- Notice emotional charge, such as a shift in tone, tears welling up, a sudden heaviness, or even a flash of defensiveness, as these signals indicate you've touched something meaningful.

- Pay attention to the body. If you ask, "Where do you feel that belief in your body?" and they can locate it immediately, the belief runs deep. This recognition can help clients feel validated and deepen their understanding of their own experience.

Mindset shifts

- Silence. A pause often means they're seeing something new. Resist the urge to fill it.

- Language of discovery: "Huh," "I never thought of it that way," "That's interesting," or "Wait..."

- A visible softening in their face, shoulders, or posture can indicate a shift. Noticing these cues helps coaches validate breakthroughs and build confidence.

- They try the new perspective on, repeating it back to themselves or rephrasing it in their own words.

- Laughter or a sudden exhale of relief, especially after naming something they've been carrying for a long time.

Signs You Need to Stay Longer

- When clients articulate a limiting belief but keep defending it or explaining why it's true.
- They understand the new perspective intellectually, but it hasn't landed emotionally. You'll hear things like "I know I shouldn't think that way, but..." or "That makes sense, but...".
- They're still using "should" language about the shift itself: "I should stop believing that."
- When the energy stays flat or the insight feels superficial, the insight hasn't taken hold yet; look for emotional resonance or spark to determine readiness to pivot.
- They circle back to the old story within a few minutes of naming the new one.

When and How to Pivot

Move from Insight to Tactics when:

- They can name the mental shift in their own words, clearly and simply
- You see or hear genuine energy behind the new perspective, not just intellectual agreement
- They've moved from "I know I should see it differently" to "I actually see it differently now."
- They start naturally asking "how" questions or talking about what they want to do next
- The insight feels grounded. You sense it could hold up outside the room, not evaporate the moment the conversation ends.

Use clarifying statements and questions like these to pivot to the Tactics phase:

- "So the shift you're making is from [old belief] to [new belief]. Does that capture it?"

- "That feels like a big realization. What would it look like to actually live from that place?"
- "Now that you're seeing it this way, what feels possible that didn't before?"
- "What would help you hold onto this when things get hard?" (This is your bridge question into Tactics)

CHAPTER 13

Tactics

Purpose

T his is the brainstorming phase. Before your client commits to specific actions, you want to explore the full range of ways they could move toward their vision. What approaches might work? What paths are available? The goal is to generate possibilities, not lock anything in yet.

With executive clients, I often compare this phase to the early stages of strategic planning, a process they know well. Except instead of building a plan for the business, they're building one for themselves: what are the key levers that will move the needle on their Vision? With athletes, this is often about previously neglected components of a comprehensive training plan: strength, speedwork, recovery, and rest. When coaching friends through life transitions, I usually talk about the weekly rhythm: what are the key areas of their life they need to attend to each week to feel more balanced, fulfilled, or aligned with their Vision?

You're aiming to land on two or three approaches that feel inspiring and exciting to try. (In a shorter conversation, even one is enough.) Notice that word: *try*. These aren't commitments or guarantees. They're experiments. Some will feel great, some won't, but all of it is valuable information. You'll define specific actions in the next phase.

Here, you're focused on the bigger picture: what paths forward might work for them?

One more thing: I always aim to include at least one approach that's mindset-related. How will they anchor the insight they just had? What will they do to reinforce the new way of thinking? Without that piece, behavioral changes often don't stick.

Questions

Questions that bridge from Insight:

- "What does that insight open up for you?"
- "If the thought that [name the new belief] became your default way of thinking, what would be possible?"
- "What strategies would help you anchor this new belief?"
- "What will you do to remind yourself of this new way of seeing things?"
- "How will you keep this insight alive when things get hard?"
- "What practices or habits would help you reinforce this new belief?"

Opening questions to generate possibilities:

- "What are some things you might like to try to achieve this vision?"
- "If you were designing a plan to make this happen, what would be in it?"
- "What needs to change for you to move toward what you want?"
- "What would have to be true about your day, week, or life for this vision to feel achievable?"

Questions that draw on what they've learned about themselves:

- "Has there ever been a time in your life when you did [reflect their goal], even in small ways? What did that look like?"
- "Think about a time when you did feel [the way they want to feel]. What allowed that to happen? What was different then?"
- "When have you been at your best in a similar situation? What were you doing?"

Questions that invite outside perspectives:

- "Do you know anyone for whom this comes easily? What do you notice about them?"
- "Imagine a person who has already achieved this goal. What are they doing yearly, quarterly, monthly, weekly, daily?"
- "What advice would you give a friend, your child, or a colleague about what to do in a similar situation?"

Questions that shift their focus forward:

- "Pick a point in the future when you've achieved this goal–6 months, a year, 5 years. What concrete changes will you have made?"
- "Which aspects of this could you pay more attention to going forward that you might overlook today?"
- "What's the smallest thing you could do that would make the biggest difference?"
- "If you could only focus on one or two things, what would have the most impact?"

Calibrating questions (especially effective when they're stuck or having a hard time coming up with ideas):

- "On a scale of 1-10, how would you rate [relevant area of their life: team cohesion, emotional health, fitness, relationships,

- stress, rest, etc.]? What's working well? What would move it closer to a 10?"
- "If you had to pick just one area to focus on first, which would make everything else easier?"
- "What feels most doable right now?"

What to Look and Listen For
When they're generating good options:
- Their energy stays high. They're engaged, leaning in, building on their own ideas.
- They start using "I could..." language rather than "I should..." This signals they're exploring from a place of possibility rather than obligation.
- They naturally connect strategies back to their vision, without you having to remind them.
- They come up with ideas that feel specific and concrete rather than vague or generic.

When they've landed on the right strategies:
- Watch for a shift in their sense of resourcefulness and empowerment. When they describe a strategy, and you see them light up, sit taller, or speak with more confidence, that's the signal.
- They stop adding new ideas. When you ask "What else?" and they pause, then say "I think that's it," you can usually trust that. You've likely found what matters most.
- They can articulate why each strategy connects to their vision. If they can't explain the link, it might not be the right fit.
- They express genuine curiosity about trying the strategy, not just willingness. You want to hear "I'm excited to see what happens" rather than "I guess I could try that."

Signs You Need to Stay Longer

- They're generating a long list of tactics, but none of them feel energizing. This often means they're operating from what they "should" do rather than genuine motivation.
- The strategies feel overwhelming or like quick fixes rather than sustainable experiments.
- You hear a lot of hedging: "Maybe I could..." or "I don't know if this would work, but..." This suggests they don't yet believe in the ideas.
- The strategies are all behavioral, with nothing addressing the mindset shift. Without a way to anchor the new belief, action items often fizzle.

When and How to Pivot

Move from Tactics to Action when:

- They've landed on two or three key strategies (or one, if you're working in a shorter timeframe) that feel both inspiring and doable.
- The strategies connect clearly to both their vision and the insight they uncovered.
- You've included at least one mindset-related strategy to begin building the shift to a more helpful mental habit.
- When you ask calibrating questions like "On a scale of 1-10, how excited are you to try this?", they're at least a 6 for at least one or two strategies.
- They start getting specific about how they'd actually do it. This is the natural bridge into Action.

Clarifying statements and questions to pivot to the Action phase:

- "So it sounds like the key strategies you want to try are [list them]. Does that feel right?"
- "You seem most energized about [specific strategy]. What would it look like to actually try that this week?"

- "Now that we have these possibilities, let's get specific. What's the next right thing to try?" (This is your bridge question into Action)

CHAPTER 14

Action

Purpose

By this phase, clients are typically energized and ready to take on the world. Your role is to channel that momentum into specific, achievable actions. I often call these actions the "best next things." Not the perfect thing or the ultimate solution, but the very next step they could take to move forward. This might be one conversation where they show up differently, one meeting where they try a new approach, one mantra to practice during a workout.

Real change happens one step at a time. When clients take small, aligned actions and experience success, their brains start to believe the new way of thinking is actually possible. Each small action becomes evidence that contradicts the old limiting belief and reinforces the latest insight. This builds momentum.

The key is helping clients design actions that balance two critical elements: the action needs to be enough of a stretch that it creates actual growth (they'll need to do something new, and new is often uncomfortable), but it also needs to be likely to happen (not so significant or scary that they won't follow through). A super shy client shouldn't commit to giving a keynote speech as their first action. Instead, maybe they speak up once at their next team meeting or share one idea in a smaller group. Your job is to help clients resist the temptation to overcommit when they're feeling inspired, and instead guide them toward the best next thing: the action that will actually happen, creating a foundation for the next step and confidence in their new ability.

When insights become embodied through action, clients create feedback loops that either reinforce their new way of thinking or reveal what needs adjustment. Either outcome is valuable. That's what the Learning phase will explore.

Questions to Ask:
Identifying the next step
- "Of everything we've talked about today, what feels like the most important place to start?"
- "What's one specific action you want to take this week related to [the insight/vision]?"
- "What's the best next thing you could do to test out this new way of thinking?"
- "If you could only do one thing differently over the next week, what would create the most momentum?"

Making it concrete
- "Let's make that really specific. When do you want to try this? Walk me through it"
- "Imagine yourself in that moment. What do you see yourself actually doing or saying? How will you set yourself up well to show up that way?"
- "How will you know you've done it? What would a fly on the wall see if they were watching?"

Testing the stretch/likely balance
- "On a scale of 1-10, how doable does this feel?"
- "What would move that number up by one point? Could this be smaller and still feel meaningful?"

- "I want this next step to be both enough of a stretch for you to try something new but also not too much of a stretch that it is too big or scary to try. How have we done in striking that balance?"
- "Does this feel challenging enough for you to learn something new from it?"

Checking alignment
- "Is this action aligned with the vision you described earlier?"
- "Does this feel inspiring to you, or does it feel like something you 'should' do?"
- "When you imagine taking this action, what do you notice in your body?"

Anticipating obstacles
- "What might get in the way of taking this action?"
- "How will you handle that when it shows up?"
- "What's your backup plan if circumstances change?"
- "What have you learned about yourself from past commitments that might be relevant here?"

Building accountability and support
- "What support do you need to make this happen?"
- "Who needs to know about this commitment?"
- "How will you remind yourself why this matters?"
- "When will we check back in about how this went?"
- "What's your plan for celebrating when you do this?"

What to Look and Listen For:

Commitment Language Clients will often use language like "I could try to…" while they're still ideating, and stronger language like "I'll plan to," or even "I will…" when they've landed on an action that feels right for them. When I hear things like "I could try…" or "I could maybe…" I will usually name it and pose a clarifying question like, "You sound hesitant. How realistic is that?" As soon as they say "I will…" or "I plan to…" I will usually clarify with, "Okay great, it sounds like you're committing to …."

Specificity You want them to move beyond vaguely defined aspirational behaviors to something that can be measured, defined and will be clear when it happens. "I'll be more assertive" isn't actionable. "I'll share one idea in Thursday's team meeting before the third person speaks" is concrete enough to create real accountability.

The Confidence Sweet Spot If a client rates their confidence at 5 or below, the action is probably too big or too vague. If they rate it above 9, it might not be enough of a stretch to create meaningful growth. Aim for that 6-8 range where they're slightly uncomfortable but still believe they can do it.

Signs You Need to Stay Longer

- The action is vague or abstract rather than specific and concrete.
- Their confidence rating is at or below 5, suggesting the action is too ambitious.
- They can't articulate when, where, or how they'll take the action.
- The action doesn't connect back to their vision or insight.
- They haven't considered how to handle potential obstacles.

When and How to Pivot:

You'll know it's time to move to Learning when:

- The client has identified a specific, concrete action with a clear timeline.
- Their confidence level is in that 6-8 range (challenging but doable).
- They've thought through potential obstacles and have strategies to handle them.
- The action clearly connects to their vision and insight from earlier in the conversation.
- You sense genuine commitment rather than compliance.

Clarifying statements and questions to pivot to the Learning phase:

- "So you're committing to [specific action] by [specific time]. Is that right?"
- "What do you think you might learn about yourself by trying this?"
- "How will you evaluate whether it has worked/is working?"
- "How will you celebrate this win?"

CHAPTER 15

Learning

Purpose

While only one element of The VITAL coaching model is called Learning, in reality, the whole point of coaching is learning. Vision, Insight, Tactics, and Action are all vehicles for helping clients along the path of self-discovery. When you ask the questions that invite people to have insights about themselves, the abstract becomes personal. That's where coaching becomes truly powerful: when you guide clients from self-discovery toward self-mastery.

> **There is challenge in change,**
> **and there is change in challenge.**

Anything worth pursuing will stretch your client in some way, and that stretch always contains something to learn. Even when an action doesn't go as planned (especially when it doesn't go as planned), there's insight waiting to be uncovered. Your role in this phase is to help clients mine their experience for what it revealed about who they are and who they're becoming.

One of the most powerful questions in this phase is simply: "Where else in your life does that apply?" This question reveals the universal beneath the specific. Someone might come in thinking they learned something about managing a difficult direct report. But when you ask where else that applies, suddenly they're seeing a pattern about how they handle conflict with anyone they perceive as challenging their authority. Their teenager. Their business partner. Their own inner critic. The specific action becomes a doorway to broader self-knowledge.

And because you're asking rather than telling, you're letting the client make the connection themselves. You're not saying "I notice this pattern seems to show up in your marriage too." You're creating space for them to discover that, which makes it stick. This question can also organically elevate the work. What started as a tactical goal ("communicate better with my team") might evolve into something more fundamental ("understand why I lash out when I feel questioned"). The learning becomes the soil for a richer vision.

Envision The VITAL coaching model as a circle. In your very first conversation with someone or in a one-off coaching moment (a hallway check-in, a single mentoring session, a quick conversation on the sidelines), you will start with Vision and end with Learning questions. For example: "What do you hope to learn about yourself by taking this action?"

But in an ongoing coaching relationship, you'll both begin and end with Learning. So in reality the conversation looks more like L-V-I-T-A-L. You'll start the conversation by referring back to what they set out to do: the action they committed to, the tactic it was part of, and the vision it serves. Then spend a few minutes on what they were able to do, acknowledging those key wins, and asking what they learned about themselves from doing that.

This also applies to what they set out to do that they didn't do. There is so much to learn from that as well. Maybe the action item was too much of a stretch. Maybe it wasn't as motivating to them as they originally thought. Maybe they are stuck because of some deeply ingrained limiting belief. Often, that learning can slightly reshape the vision and almost always informs the next action items.

Learning isn't a separate phase tacked on at the end. It's the connection that makes The VITAL coaching model a loop rather than a line. Learning is both the destination and the starting point of each subsequent coaching conversation.

This is also where the cumulative power of coaching becomes visible. Over time, clients don't just solve individual problems. They develop a clearer relationship with themselves. They start to recognize their own patterns, anticipate their own resistance, and trust their own capacity to grow. That's self-mastery. And it happens one learning conversation at a time.

Questions

When you're in the Action phase and your client has just committed to trying something new (these questions help them approach the action with curiosity rather than a pass/fail mindset):

- "What would you like to learn about yourself by doing this?"
- "How will you know if your action is working? What will you notice?"
- "What do you want to pay attention to this week as you try this?"
- "When will you check in with yourself about how this went?"
- "What's one question you want to keep asking yourself between now and when we talk next?"

When opening a follow-up coaching conversation:
Start by referring back to what they set out to do:

- "Last time we talked, you decided to try [action item] as part of [strategy] in service of your overall goal to [vision]. Let's start with what you set out to do that you were able to do."

- "What went well?"

Acknowledging key wins:

Before moving into deeper learning, take time to genuinely acknowledge what they accomplished. Don't rush past the wins to get to the "work." Celebration matters. When someone takes a risk, even a small one, honoring that reinforces the new belief system they're building.

- "That's a real accomplishment. How does it feel to have done that?"
- "What does it mean to you that you were able to follow through on this?"
- "I want to pause here because what you just described is a huge win."

Connecting the dots:

This is where you help them connect the dots between what they did and what they now understand about themselves:

- "What did you learn about yourself from doing this hard thing?"
- "What does this tell you about what you're capable of?"
- "What belief did this experience confirm or challenge?"
- "When you've been able to successfully do something like this in the past, what did you learn about yourself then that we can draw from now?"
- "What did you notice as you tried this new approach?"
- "What surprised you?"
- "What was harder or easier than you expected?"

Expanding the learning:
- "Where else in your life does this apply?"
- "What other relationships/situations would benefit from this learning?"

When they didn't do what they set out to do:
This is where many coaches get anxious. But the truth is, not doing something is equally valuable data. I often say, "Awesome! Let's get curious about that." Then I ask solution-focused questions that help hone in on what they might want to try going forward:
- "What do you make of that?"
- "What do you think would have enabled you to do that?"
- "Was the action too ambitious? Or was it the wrong approach entirely?"
- "How would you like to try it differently next time?"
- "What did you learn about yourself from not doing it?"
- "Is there a smaller version of this you could try?"
- "What felt true about the intention, even if the execution didn't happen?"

Closing a single conversation:
Even in a one-off conversation, you can invite reflection at the end:
- "What did you learn about yourself in our conversation today?"
- "What's the biggest thing you're taking away from this?"
- "What shifted for you?"
- "What feels different now than when we started?"

What to Look and Listen For
The quality of their reflection:
Are they reflecting on what happened, or what it means? Surface-level learning sounds like "I learned that meetings are hard." Deeper learning sounds like "I learned that I shut down when I feel

dismissed." Help them move from the event to the pattern to the self-discovery.

Connection to identity:
The most powerful learning moments happen when someone connects an action to who they are becoming. Listen for statements like "I guess I'm someone who can actually do this" or "Maybe I've been telling myself the wrong story." These are golden opportunities. Pause and acknowledge the significance.

Energy shifts:
When someone lands on genuine insight about themselves, you'll feel the energy shift. They might get quiet and reflective, or they might light up with recognition. Either way, slow down and stay with it. Don't rush to the next question.

Resistance or deflection:
Sometimes clients will minimize their wins ("It wasn't a big deal") or gloss over what they didn't do ("I just got busy"). Gently bring them back with curiosity towards deeper reflection. Both the wins and the non-actions contain important information.

Patterns emerging:
As you work with someone over time, you'll start to notice themes in what they learn. They might consistently struggle with the same kind of obstacle, or consistently surprise themselves in the same way. Reflecting those patterns back can be powerful.

Signs You Need to Stay Longer
- They're describing what happened but not what it means.
- They're dismissing or minimizing their progress.

- They seem defensive about what didn't go as planned.
- The reflection feels performative rather than genuine.

When and How to Pivot

In an ongoing relationship, you'll know it's time to cycle back to Vision when:

- They've learned something meaningful about themselves.
- The learning has revealed something new they want to work on.
- You hear them naturally start talking about "what's next" or "what I want now".
- There's a clear thread from what they learned to where they want to go.
- The energy shifts from reflective to forward-looking.

Clarifying statements and questions to pivot back to Vision:

- "Given what you've learned, what feels most important to focus on now?"
- "How does this inform what you want to work on?"
- "It sounds like this experience surfaced something new. Where do you want to take it?"
- "What does this make you want to go after next?"

In a one-off conversation, Learning is your closing. You'll know you're done when:

- They can articulate what they're taking away.
- The insight feels grounded and personal, not abstract.
- They seem settled, clear, or energized rather than confused or scattered.

Clarifying statements and questions to close:

- "What's the one thing you want to hold onto from our conversation?"

- "It sounds like you're walking away with some real clarity. Is there anything else you need before we wrap up?"
- "You came in thinking about [X], and now you're seeing [Y]. That's a meaningful shift."

It Starts with You

If you've made it this far, you now know something that most people who call themselves coaches, managers, mentors, and leaders never learn: the most powerful way to help someone change isn't to give them the answer. It's to ask the questions that help them find their own.

This isn't just a philosophy. It's how the brain actually works.

Every person you'll ever coach has a brain that's been uniquely wired by their lived experience. Your solution, no matter how brilliant, won't fix their problem. When people feel like someone is telling them what to do, they can easily feel judged, unseen, or worse, unimportant. Their defenses go up, and their powers of critical and creative thinking go down. But when they have their own "aha" moments through powerful questioning, they build new beliefs that stick. They don't just change their behavior temporarily because they feel their back is against the wall. They change how they see themselves, others, their work, and the world.

That's the difference between telling people what to do and helping them think for themselves.

You've learned the science behind why this works. You've learned the four practices: regarding clients as resourceful and whole, asking instead of telling, focusing on solutions rather than problems, and listening generously. You've walked through The VITAL coaching model and seen how Vision leads to Insight, Insight opens up Tactics, Tactics become Action, Action feeds Learning, and Learning opens up possibilities for a vision of their life and career better than they ever thought possible.

But here's what I want you to remember most: the practices in this book aren't just techniques. They're ways of being. You can't create the conditions for someone else's best thinking while your own mind is cluttered with urgency, judgment, or the need to prove your value. The change has to start with you.

That means noticing when you're about to jump in with advice and choosing curiosity instead. It means trusting that the person in front of you has wisdom you can't see yet. It means getting comfortable with silence, with not knowing, with the slower pace of real discovery. It means managing your own humanity so that you can work with theirs.

This will feel awkward at first. It goes against our automatic tendencies. You'll catch yourself mid-sentence, realizing you're telling instead of asking. You'll want to ask "What happened?" You'll forget to ask "What else?" You'll slip into the details and drama of a problem because it's so deeply ingrained. That's okay. That's the work.

The goal isn't perfection. It's practice. Every conversation is a chance to get a little better at creating the conditions for ownership, insight, and action.

And when you watch someone's face light up as they see something they couldn't see before, when they say "I never thought of it that way" or "Oh... that's what's been going on," you'll understand why this matters. You'll see that you didn't give them that insight. You created the space for them to find it themselves. And because they found it, it belongs to them. It will travel with them long after your conversation ends.

Over time, the people you coach won't just solve their immediate problems. They'll develop a clearer relationship with themselves. They'll start to recognize their own patterns, anticipate their own resistance, and trust their own capacity to grow. They'll need you less. That's not a failure of your coaching. That's the whole point. Self-mastery means they've internalized what you helped them discover. They can access their own answers now.

And they'll remember you as the person who helped them get there. Not because you had all the answers, but because you asked the questions that unlocked theirs.

That's your legacy.

You have everything you need to start. And the best way to learn this is by doing it.

Now go have a conversation that changes someone's life.

ABOUT THE AUTHOR

Jenn Farrer is an executive coach certified by the International Coaching Federation and the NeuroLeadership Institute, and a running coach certified by the Road Runners Club of America. She is also an award-winning researcher in the field of communication, collaboration, and influence. She has worked with thousands of executives, athletes, and teams as a coach, trainer, and speaker on the topics of leadership, coaching skills, and personal performance. Her writing has been published in *Forbes* and the *Huffington Post*.

At 26, Jenn survived a life-threatening stroke. In the aftermath, she woke up to her own limiting beliefs about achievement and worthiness, beliefs she couldn't have seen while she was in them. No one could have told her what needed to change. She had to discover it for herself. That experience shapes everything about how she coaches today.

She splits her time between New York City and the North Fork of Long Island, where she lives with her husband, son, and two cats.

www.ingramcontent.com/pod-product-compliance
Lightning Source LLC
Chambersburg PA
CBHW071222090426
42736CB00014B/2942